Cracking The Thinking Skills Assessment

This textbook is the property of Mitesh Desai. Any attempt to copy or distribute this booklet without his express permission will be considered a breach of copyright law and may result in prosecution.

Contents

Page	Description
3	Foreword
4	Exam Overview
5	An Important Note on Strategy
6	Verbal Reasoning – Active VS Passive Reading
7	TSA Passages
8	Identifying Assumptions
11	Strengthening/Weakening Arguments
14	Spotting Flaws in Arguments
17	Identifying and Drawing Conclusions
19	Numerical Reasoning – Introduction
20	Mental Maths Drill
21	Areas and Volumes
25	Fractions
28	Percentages/Proportions
31	Probability
34	Speed/Distance/Time
36	Data in tables/graphs
39	Shapes/Spaces
43	Practice Questions – Numerical
59	Practice Questions – Verbal
86	Answers to Practice Questions – Numerical
106	Answers to Practice Questions - Verbal

Foreword

If you are reading this then you have decided to apply to Oxford or Cambridge (Oxbridge) for a course which requires completion of the Thinking Skills Assessment (TSA).

Unless you have completed the GMAT, The TSA is unlike any exam you have completed to date. The exam tests a small number of very simple concepts but does so in subtle and complicated ways. One of the most important things to remember at the start of this course is that handling the concepts well will only get you part of the way towards achieving a very high score. The other side of the experience is coping with the time pressure. Many of the questions can absorb your attention for 5 to 10 minutes and the answer will sometimes feel like it can be reached but your problem solving skills and strategies aren't quite getting you there. It is important to realise at this point that the marginal value of this one extra mark is almost inconsequential relative to the remainder of the paper and all the marks you could score there. Guess and move on!

It should also be noted that successfully completing the TSA in itself will not be sufficient to gain entrance into Oxbridge. This is merely a yard stick which indicates ability to think laterally and understand concepts – having completed this you still need to overcome an interview! Preparation for interviews need not be taxing; read the economist every week (not cover to cover but not just one relevant section either), read the books you claim to have read in your personal statement and have an opinion which you feel able to defend on these topics - If you mention Economic Development but don't know whether you think food aid is good or bad for Africa as a whole then you've got a serious problem!

Oxbridge seem to split performance into four quartiles, so there is no "pass mark" or target score in the TSA – you simply need to outperform 24.9% of the people who apply that year in order to be in the uppermost quartile. Oxford is more likely to positively discriminate to the benefit of less privileged candidates, meaning nothing but the top quartile for private school applicants will be sufficient. To achieve this, hard work is needed from now until you complete the exam. This sacrifice of a few short months could impact not just your three years as an undergraduate but also your professional life through to middle age. Whether you are willing to demonstrate the maturity to devote the coming months entirely to your work is very much your choice. While GCSEs and AS-Levels can reward last minute cramming, this exam is very different and will punish those who are underprepared. It is simply not possible to score highly in this exam without huge amounts of practice.

Good luck,

Mitesh Desai

Exam Overview

Format: The paper is divided into two sections which in total require 2 hours to complete.

Section A: 50 Multiple Choice Questions with 90 minutes to complete (approximately this equates to 1 minute and 48 seconds per question)

Section B: Complete one essay (four titles will be presented to you) in 30 minutes.

Grading: Not negatively marked – therefore you should answer all questions

Scores are scaled using the 'rasch' method – this means harder questions earn more credit than easy ones. The key thing to take from this point is that if a single question goes wrong or even a string of questions throw you off, do not be alarmed! All is not lost! Just consistently focus on the next question – this exam is designed to ensure that most students get quite a lot of questions wrong. To answer even 35 of the questions correctly in Section A will lead to a potentially strong score. The feeling of completing an exam knowing you're only hoping to score 70% will be a strange sensation for many of you.

Skills tested: Numerical Reasoning

   Verbal Reasoning

Numerical Reasoning:

This involves nothing beyond GCSE maths

Key concepts: Fractions

   Percentages

   Measurements (e.g. Area and Volume)

Also tested: Spatial Awareness

   Understanding information presented in tables/graphs

Verbal Reasoning:

This is focussed entirely on arguments

Key concepts: Identifying conclusions

   Identifying assumptions

   Spotting flaws in an argument

   Weaken or strengthen arguments

   Identify parallel reasoning

An important note on strategy

The exam presents the numerical and verbal questions in a jumbled fashion, the first question in the exam could be testing your verbal reasoning but the second and third might be focussed on numerical skills. It would require more effort to keep switching and adapting and so for this reason it is essential when completing this exam that you first complete ALL the verbal questions and following this move onto the numerical questions.

Over time and with practice you will tend to complete the verbal section faster which is why I recommend completing this section first, but some of you will prefer to tackle the numerical section first instead. The key is that you deal with a single type of question before moving onto the second type. This will increase your efficiency and also help you to find answers quicker.

Verbal Reasoning

Active vs Passive Reading

"Ethanol, a fuel derived from corn, can be used alone to power cars or along with gasoline to reduce the amount of gas' consumed. Unlike gasoline, ethanol is easily renewable since it is primarily converted from the sun's energy. Moreover, compared with conventional gasoline, ethanol is a cleaner burning fuel. To save energy and reduce pollution, many individuals advocate the increased usage of ethanol as a primary fuel source in conjunction with or in place of gasoline."

> 1. What is this paragraph about?

This question is easy enough, right? "Ethanol" or "Renewable energy" would be suitable responses to this question. Sadly the TSA does not make life so easy.

> 2. What structure is this paragraph in?

To answer this question many of you will have to read the passage again. Having done so, some of you may still struggle! To effectively answer this question, a focus on the keywords is essential. Don't be fooled into thinking that the keywords relate to the subject matter; the subject matter in the TSA is largely based on material which candidates won't know much about precisely because the exam wishes to test your understanding of <u>arguments</u> NOT your understanding of renewable energy!

How keywords can help us to read actively

Have you ever read a paragraph then half way through realised you have no idea what you just read? When approaching the TSA, this is a mistake you simply cannot afford because of the time constraints. The trick in the exam is to not get lost in the details contained in the paragraph but instead to use keywords to anticipate what material is coming in each sentence. Doing so will make you a more active reader and help you to answer questions quickly and correctly.

Without focussing on the actual subject matter do you see that:

Sentence one: Introduces a topic, *"Ethanol"*

Sentence two: Identifies a difference between ethanol and gas

Sentence three: Identifies another difference between ethanol and gas

Sentence four: Concludes the argument.

Now having seen that, answer the following question: *What is the impact of these two keywords in the passage above?*

1. Unlike

2. Moreover

Do you see how understanding the impact of these words at the beginning of the sentence can actually make the content easier to digest? Spotting these words as you read will help you anticipate the information which is about to be presented and make you realise that the content itself is not as important as understanding the nature of the information you have been presented with.

It is clear that "unlike" at the start of the second sentence tells us that a difference between Gasoline and Ethanol is about to be presented. "Moreover" is a synonym for "furthermore" and tells us that another difference is coming up. Being able to spot these keywords and anticipate what information is coming will help you to read actively and also will save you valuable time as with practice you will save a great deal of time when you don't have to read passages more than once.

Passages

Many TSA questions (typically in the past, 25 out of 50 in Section A) will begin with a passage of information on some topic. While these paragraphs will be quite varied in terms of subject material, the skills being tested are in fact very simple.

Broadly, all arguments in the TSA will be composed of the following:

1. **Evidence** – Oxford graduates earn more than Cambridge graduates

2. **A conclusion (based on the evidence)** – Therefore, Oxford is better than Cambridge

3. **An assumption** – This is always unstated.

The assumption is critical for success in the TSA. To find correct answers we will consistently need to be able to work out what the assumption is.

So what is the assumption above?

Most likely it is that "Earnings are a good determinant of the quality of education one has received". Predicting assumptions is important because having done this it becomes very easy to "knock-out" incorrect answer choices in difficult questions, or spot correct answers in easier questions.

As we focus in on each type of question this page can be constantly referred to as a reminder of the simple components of each TSA passage and what we are really looking for when we read these convoluted and confusing passages of information!

Question Styles – Verbal Reasoning

We will focus on the main questions which tend to come up in the TSA, namely:

- Identifying assumptions
- Strengthening/Weakening arguments
- Spotting flaws in arguments
- Identifying and drawing conclusions
- Parallel Reasoning

1. Identifying Assumptions

As previously mentioned, identifying assumptions is key for success on the TSA. Many questions on the TSA will simply ask you to specifically identify the assumption. The key focus has to be on working out what the evidence and conclusion are in order to connect the two using an assumption. Let's look at some examples to kick us off:

In each of these sentences, underline the evidence and denote it with an "e", underline the conclusion and denote it with a "c", then write down what the assumption is that connects the evidence to the conclusion.

e.g. Adam's favourite fruit pastille is one which is red coloured. Therefore, he also likes red coloured skittles best.

This is the evidence; it may not be clear from this sentence alone but the next sentence will make it abundantly clear	This is a conclusion. It is based on the preceding evidence. The word "therefore" makes it very clear that a conclusion is coming before you've even read this sentence (Think: Keyword!)

The assumption in the above argument might be that, "red fruit pastilles are the same flavour as red skittles"

You may have thought of a different assumption to the one above. That is perfectly fine as long as it connects the evidence to the conclusion (e.g. fruit pastilles are similar to skittles). Sometimes your initial assumption will be shaped by the answer choices the TSA gives you.

Task: Identify the evidence and the conclusion from the statements below. Then think of at least one assumption that might link the two.

1. Teachers tend to be more productive straight after the holiday. Therefore, the break must be relaxing for them.

2. Exposure to radioactive material can cause radioactive poisoning and death. Thus generation of power by harnessing nuclear energy must be banned.

(Look back at these two sentences; did you spot the keywords? "Thus" and "Therefore". What do these words tell you is coming?)

Now let's look at some past exam questions and review the technique for solving them:

> When news periodicals begin forecasting a recession, people tend to spend less money on non-essential purchases. Therefore, the perceived threat of a future recession decreases the willingness of people to purchase products that they regard as optional or luxury goods.
>
> *Which of the following is an assumption on which the argument depends?*
>
> a) People do not always agree as to which goods should be considered luxury goods
> b) People are more likely to have read a news periodical recently because more and more periodicals are being published
> c) Most people do not regularly read news periodicals
> d) The consumer perception of the threat of recession increases when news periodicals begin forecasting a recession
> e) At least some of the biggest spending consumers prior to the recession were among those who curtailed their spending after the recession began.

So let's review the strategy:

> 1. **Read the question**
> Reading the question before you start to look at the paragraph will help set your mind up to look for the key information. Each TSA question requires a slightly different skillset and preparing yourself to look for the key information before you look at each passage will stop you reading paragraphs over and over again and save you time.
>
> 2. **Identify the conclusion**
> Is there a keyword which gives away the conclusion? "Therefore" is a word which often connects a preceding line of evidence to a new thought in the TSA. Typically that new thought will be the conclusion.
>
> In this case, the conclusion reads, "Therefore, the perceived threat of a future recession decreases the willingness of people to purchase products that they regard as optional or luxury goods"
>
> 3. **Identify the evidence**
> It is very likely that what came before this conclusion is the evidence, in this case, "When news periodicals begin forecasting a recession, people tend to spend less money on non-essential purchases"
>
> 4. **Predict the assumption**
> What assumption connects these two? Perhaps that the newspaper reporting the risk of a recession makes consumers think a recession is more likely?
>
> 5. **Evaluate the answer choices**

> For a question like this, all we really need is to find an answer which looks somewhat similar to our prediction in the step before.
>
> Choice (a) might be true but isn't relevant. This argument isn't about whether people agree on what constitutes a luxury good it is about spending on them. Since this answer is out of scope it is wrong.
>
> Choice (b) this could strengthen the conclusion but doesn't reflect what the assumption is. Thus it is wrong too.
>
> Choice (c) would weaken the conclusion drawn but again, doesn't reflect what the assumption is.
>
> Choice (d) almost perfectly matches our prediction and is correct.
>
> Choice (e) this answer is focussed on a past recession but the argument presented is focussed on a future recession. Again, it is incorrect.

Sometimes the assumption you predict won't match any of the answer choices. In this case you need to be flexible – you might not have thought of all the possible assumptions between some evidence and the conclusion.

When none of the answer choices seem appealing (or when all of them do!) then you need to start knocking out answers. Above you can see reasons why I have ruled out each answer. With practice you will also get comfortable doing the same.

Task: Go through the question section at the back of this textbook and attempt all the "Find the assumption" questions.

Key points:

1. It is absolutely essential that you complete the questions without looking at the answer section. During the exam you won't have the comfort of an answer section so you have to get used to dealing with this new style of question without constantly looking at the answers.
2. The questions are purposely unordered. It is important that you get used to reading questions and determining what skill the TSA wants to examine. Having to sort through the questions by yourself will improve this skill.

2. Strengthening/Weakening arguments

These two ideas get lumped together because answering these questions really requires the same skills.

The strategy to answer these questions is broadly the same as the previous questions. Let's look at the same examples again and think about what ideas might strengthen them.

e.g. Adam's favourite fruit pastille is one which is red coloured. Therefore, he also likes red coloured skittles best.

Previously we identified the evidence and conclusion in the argument above. This time however, we need to think about what might strengthen the argument. To do so, we need to think again about the unstated assumption which connects the two ideas. Once we have a sense for what the assumption might be, to strengthen the argument we simply need to identify an answer which makes the assumption more likely to be true.

Previously we said the assumption might be that red pastilles and red skittles are the same flavour.

So, to strengthen this argument we would want to pick an answer choice which makes this assumption more likely to be true.

Now let's look at some exam style questions and review the technique for solving them:

At Google, many employees quit recently and took jobs at rival firms. Shortly before the employees quit, Google lost its largest client. Clearly, the employees are no longer confident in Google's long-term viability.

Which of the following, if true, most strengthens the argument?

(a) Employees leaving Google receive significant pay increases
(b) Google's largest client accounted for 60% of its profits
(c) Many candidates, having received an offer from Google, ultimately accepted jobs elsewhere
(d) Recently many employees have complained of poor work-life balance working at Google
(e) Many employees had signed contracts with their new employers long before Google lost the client

---

Let's use virtually the same strategy as last time to solve this question:

---

1. Identify the conclusion
Once again a keyword is used to make it obvious that a conclusion is coming - "Clearly". The conclusion in this instance is that "...the employees are no longer confident in Google's long term viability"

2. Identify the evidence
As before, we now pick out the evidence and find that, "...many employees quit recently and took jobs at rival firms. Shortly before the employees quit, Google lost its largest client"

3. Predict the assumption
Here, the assumption may be that employees quit because Google lost the client. This certainly connects the evidence with the conclusion.

4. Evaluate the answer choices
To strengthen this argument, we must simply pick an answer which makes the assumption we have predicted more likely. Let's see if any do this for us:

(a) This makes our assumption less likely. It provides another reason why employees are leaving Google

(b) This is tempting; it would certainly imply a big loss to Google to have lost this client

(c) This is also tempting but it is a trap answer! The argument is about current employees, not potential employees. Therefore this answer is incorrect

(d) This answer weakens the argument that workers are leaving Google because it's a sinking ship – it gives an alternative explanation which doesn't help us answer this question

(e) Once again this weakens the assumption; it orders events in a way that the loss of the client could not explain the decision of workers to leave Google

So here (b) is the best answer. Note that it isn't the perfect answer but it's better than the other four choices we have. Sometimes the TSA requires us to cherry pick the most appealing answer instead of consistently presenting us with the perfect answer.

For the sake of clarity let's also have a look at a weaken question:

CEO: Over the past several years, we have more than doubled our revenues but profits have steadily declined because an increasing number of customers have failed to pay their balances. In order to compensate for these higher default rates we will increase the interest charged on outstanding balances from an annual percentage rate (APR) of 9.5% to an APR of 12%. This increase will be sufficient to compensate for the current rate of defaults and allow us to increase our profits.

Which of the following statements, if true, would most seriously undermine a plan to increase interest rates in order to spur profitable growth?

(a) Many other companies have experienced a similar trend in their default rates
(b) The company's operating expenses are above the industry average and can be substantially reduced, thus increasing margins
(c) The increase in default rates was due to a rise in unemployment, but unemployment rates are expected to drop in the coming months.
(d) The proposed increase in the APR will, alone, more than double the company's profit margins
(e) An increase in the APR charged on credit card balances often results in higher rates of default.

Let's use exactly the same strategy as we did for the previous "strengthen" question with one small tweak:

1. Identify the conclusion
Here the conclusion is masked within two sentences. It is effectively "Let's increase the APR to increase our profits in the face of more defaults"

2. Identify the evidence

The evidence here is that revenues have doubled but profits are lower. This is because of the increased defaults.

3. Predict the assumption

Here the assumption is that a higher APR will increase profits.

4. Evaluate the answer choices

To weaken this argument, we must simply pick an answer which makes the assumption we have predicted less likely. Let's see if any do this for us:

(a) This is interesting but doesn't make our assumption less likely. It's not within the scope of the question.

(b) This offers an alternative solution to increase profits but doesn't really help us answer the question as it is phrased. If no better answer presents itself this may be tempting.

(c) Once again this answer provides a compelling explanation for what is going on but doesn't indicate that the CEO's plan is likely to fail.

(d) The CEO did say that the change in rates would increase the profits, so this is no surprise.

(e) This undoubtedly is the answer. If more people default then the higher APR most certainly won't increase profits.

So here (e) is the best answer.

3. Spotting flaws in arguments

The TSA will sometimes require us to find the flaw in an argument. Typically the question is phrased as "Which one of the following best identifies the flaw in the argument?" or "Which one of the following identifies the flaw in the argument above?"

Once again, the key to solving these questions is going to lie in your ability to find the evidence and conclusion in the passage. Once you have done this you can determine the assumption. Finally examine each answer choice and look for an answer which turns the assumption on its head. You can also use logic to determine which answer choice is most appropriate.

Let's look at some sample texts and see how spotting the evidence and conclusion, then determining the assumption, will help us to pick out the flaws in the argument:

> "Hugo was recovering from the flu when he visited Angela last week, and now Angela is showing signs of the flu. If Hugo had waited until he was no longer contagious, Angela would not have become ill"
>
> Let's first identify the conclusion here: "If Hugo had waited until he was no longer contagious, Angela would not have become ill"
>
> The evidence behind this conclusion is that' "Hugo was recovering from the flu when he visited Angela last week"
>
> So what is the assumption here? Does it make sense that we're assuming that Angela caught the flu off Hugo? In this instance, any answer choice which suggests that Angela may have caught the flu from someone other than Hugo will suffice.

> *Write down what you think the weaknesses are in the following arguments:*
>
> Dolphins have larger brains than humans. Therefore, dolphins are more intelligent than humans.
>
>
>
>
> Johnny has longer legs than Andy. Clearly, this explains why Johnny is a faster sprinter than Andy.

Now, have a look at this example from a past TSA exam and see how you get on:

> "The government blames schools and teachers for boys underperforming. However, science tells a different story. Evolutionary biology shows that females have evolved to have better verbal and emotional skills than males because of the need in prehistoric times for women to take the lead in child rearing. By contrast, the need for males in prehistoric times to hunt in packs for food has made males more prone to violence and also skilled at calculating and planning. Neurologists have added to this insight by showing that the male hormone testosterone has an adverse impact on language skills. So clearly differences in educational performance between boys and girls cannots be explained in terms of failing teachers."
>
> *Which of the following is the best statement of the flaw in the above argument?*
>
> (a) It assumes that scientific explanations apply to the average male or female ignoring exceptions
> (b) It assumes that biological differences come in degrees and are not absolute
> (c) It assumes that skills in calculating and planning have a role in educational performance
> (d) It assumes that the differences in performance between the sexes are due solely to biological differences
> (e) It assumes that teachers are not trying to improve the performance of failing boys
>
> The reason I have put this past exam question in here is because it is far more chunky in terms of the amount of text they give you. It is a skill in itself to extract the evidence and conclusion from so much more information. There is *a keyword* which *makes the conclusion easy to find*, "So clearly", but *the evidence is a little more tricky to pick out*. At this point you can also start to think about *paraphrasing*. Instead of trying to underline precisely what the evidence is, it might be worth paraphrasing the evidence in your mind into a short sentence. The evidence is split across a number of sentences and is effectively just "evolutionary reasons why girls would outperform boys at school"
>
> So now we have the following evidence and conclusion:
>
> Evidence: Evolutionary reasons why girls outperform boys at school
> Conclusion: Teachers aren't to blame for boys' poor performance
>
> So let's now *evaluate the answer choices* to determine whether any of them highlight the flaw in this argument.
>
> (a) This is not relevant to the question
> (b) This uses some fancy language but ultimately also fails to identify any flaw in the line of argument
> (c) The text does refer to calculation and planning but does it really imply any link between these and educational performance?
> (d) This is compelling – the text certainly does imply that biological reasons are the sole explanation of differences in performance
> (e) The argument is nothing to do with how the teachers are addressing the performance of the boys
>
> While this question requires a bit of thought, it can be clear that (d) is the best answer for this question.

Before we move on, let's group the flaws that tend to occur in the TSA into some key categories:

1. Insufficient information

This is when the passage will present you with some information but it won't be enough to support the conclusion.

e.g. Brian's income is rising despite unemployment rising. Therefore Brian is educated more than average

It could be true that Brian is earning more because he is more educated, but the passage hasn't told us this explicitly. This flaw is pretty obvious relative to questions you will face in the TSA but the key thing to pick up is the sort of flaw to look for when reading a text.

2. Generalisations

Sometimes a conclusion will capture a much larger group than the evidence itself refers to.

e.g. White tigers are more likely to attack humans. Therefore all tigers should be kept captive.

The evidence is totally focussed on white tigers but the conclusion refers to all tigers. This is an generalisation and for all we know, normal tigers are very friendly towards humans.

3. Creating a causal link between unconnected ideas

This is similar to the example we used earlier on with respect to Dolphin and Human brain sizes. Does the size of a brain really reveal how intelligent an animal is?

4. Misinterpretation

Sometimes the conclusion can misinterpret the evidence presented.

e.g. Space has been expanding infinitely since time began. Therefore a larger universe may hold the solution to the global population crisis.

The evidence here is about space but the conclusion seems focussed on the earth.

4. Identifying and drawing conclusions

Identifying and drawing conclusions are two different tasks; identifying a conclusion essentially means picking it out of the text. We have already practised this skill a number of times in our preparation for the TSA hopefully.

Drawing a conclusion requires candidates to think about the information presented and then decide what conclusion is most appropriate given the information available.

This second question in particular will require candidates to interpret the meaning of sentences. This can sometimes lead to a difference of opinion.

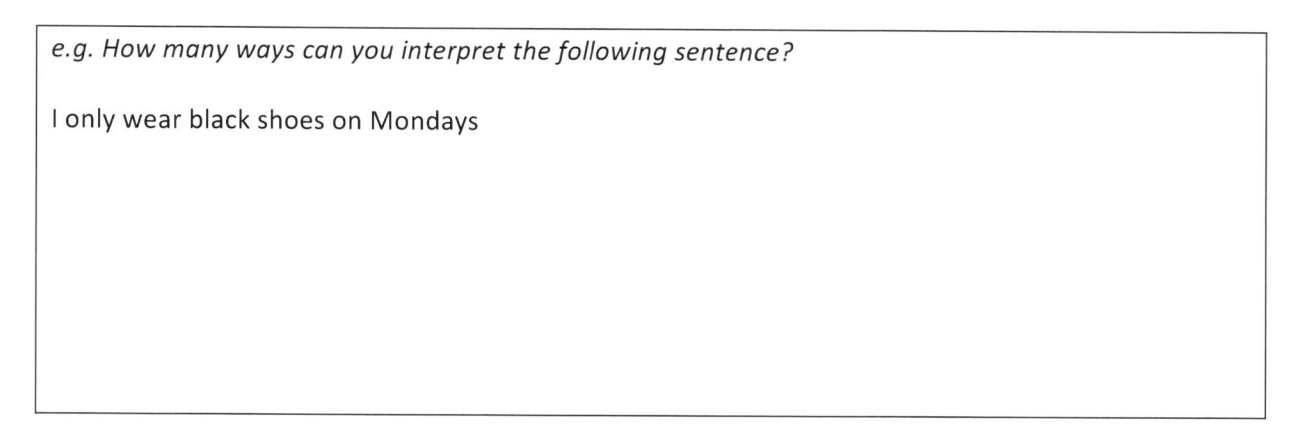

> *e.g. How many ways can you interpret the following sentence?*
>
> I only wear black shoes on Mondays

The previous sentence could imply that every day, other than Monday, you wear shoes which are not black coloured, OR it could suggest that on Mondays you wear nothing except for black shoes! With respect to the TSA the sentences in the passage which surround a sentence like this one will help you determine how to correctly interpret the sentence.

For example, if the passage read, "I only wear black shoes on Monday. The rest of the week I am based in the gym", you are now in a position to interpret that every other day the person chooses to wear trainers which aren't black.

When drawing conclusions it is important to only use the information given and to evaluate the answer choices carefully. Have a look at the next example:

> More sitcoms have been appearing on TV at an alarming rate. This has led to less diversity in terms of what appears on our televisions and to comedy programmes that contain a similar type of humour as each other. Some have criticised this trend and argued that we should resist more of these programmes from being shown on television, but, at the end of the day, television companies that produce and broadcast these sitcoms know what the majority of people want to watch
>
> *Which one of the following conclusions can reliably be drawn from the above argument?*
>
> (a) The majority of people argue that we should resist more sitcoms from being shown on television
> (b) What appears on television is affected by consumer demand
> (c) Sitcoms will continue to appear on our televisions at the same rate
> (d) Most programmes on television are now sitcoms
> (e) Calls to resist more of these programmes from appearing on television will lead to fewer sitcoms appearing

In assessing this question we need to first ensure we have digested the key points in the passage.

Broadly, the ideas conveyed are:

1. More sitcoms on TV - lots of similar shows
2. Some are against this, but TV companies know what people want to watch

Now we can start to look at the answer choices and try to knock out incorrect answers:

(a) "The majority" makes this incorrect immediately. The text says "Some"
(c) There's nothing in the paragraph to suggest whether this is true. The passage has told us that sitcoms are appearing at an alarming rate today but says nothing about the future
(d) The passage doesn't state this and it is not clear whether or not it is true
(e) We can't be sure this is true. Nothing in the passage tells us what response there has been to the "some" who have been calling for fewer sitcoms

This method leaves us only with answer choice (b) – which we have not even read yet! "What appears on television is affected by consumer demand" can most definitely be concluded from the ideas conveyed in the paragraph though. If there are more sitcoms on TV, and TV companies know what people want to watch, it is certainly possible to conclude that consumer demand will affect what shows are on TV.

Numerical Reasoning

Mathematically speaking, the concepts covered in the TSA are very straightforward; none of them go much beyond GCSE maths. Given this, many students are surprised and confused by how challenging they find the questions.

The reason the questions are so challenging is largely because of the way in which the information is presented – it is often difficult to extract all the relevant information quickly in order to solve the question. The time pressure often makes students try to over-simplify questions which will lead you into trap answers. Because the exam is multiple-choice it means there are often answers which seem appealing but a little further examination can help reveal that the answer is actually incorrect.

Broadly the topics we need to cover are as follows:

1. Areas/Volumes
2. Fractions
3. Percentages/Ratios
4. Probability
5. Speed/Distance/Time
6. Data in tables/graphs
7. Shapes and Spaces

This exam is not like completing your GCSEs or A-Levels, the questions have similar traits but are rarely repetitive. We need to focus on using new strategies which will help us complete these problems. These will include:

1. Picking numbers
2. Strategically using the answer choices to guide our thinking
3. Mathematically describing verbal problems
4. Spotting opportunities to make easy mistakes and avoiding them

The other important thing to realise is that this is a non-calculator exam. If you find yourself trying to work out some maths in your head which is extremely complicated this should sound off an alarm bell in your head – it means you're probably not doing the right calculation!

The only way to improve your speed and precision with respect to mental arithmetic is to practice. Don't let a moment alone pass by when you're not trying to work out some basic maths problems; the next page is just a series of calculations which you should be able to complete in less than 15 seconds. If you can't do it already then keep designing your own questions and testing yourself until you can.

Mental Maths Drill

Try to complete each question in less than 15 seconds:

1. 14 x 16

2. 2500 x 40

3. 100 x 100

4. The time is 3.20pm, what is the small angle between the clock hands?

5. Jill has 90 sweets, eats 3 an hour for 2 hours then gives half away. How many does she have left?

6. 87 – 29

7. 14 – 9

8. 112/14

9. 156/12

10. A restaurant serves 100 people during a working week (Monday-Friday) at a cost of $7 per plate, pays rent of $36,000 per year and pays 1 waiter $20 per day worked. What is the monthly cost to run the restaurant?

11. x% of y is 10. Y% of 120 is 48. What is x?

12. A bowl is half full of water. Four cups of water are then added to the bowl, filling the bowl to 70% of its capacity. How many cups of water are now in the bowl?

13. 800, increased by 50% and then decreased by 30% yields what number?

14. 200 is 16% of what number?

15. Express the following as a percentage: 25/8

Areas and Volumes

To very briefly remind ourselves – calculating the area of a cube is simply: **width x height**

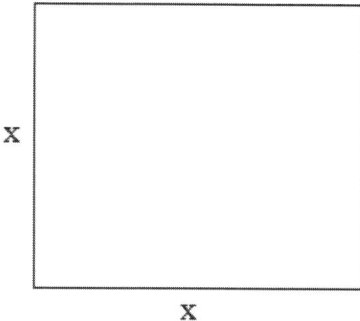

The area of a triangle is equal to **½ x base x perpendicular height**

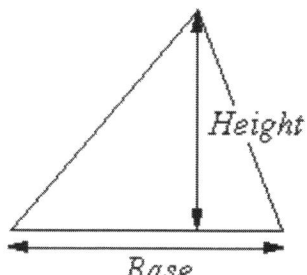

Finally, the area of a circle is equal to **πr²**. It will also be helpful to remember that the circumference of a circle is equal to 2πr

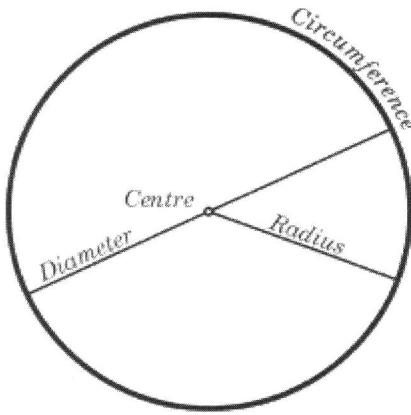

The volume of a cuboid is equal to its **width x height x depth**.

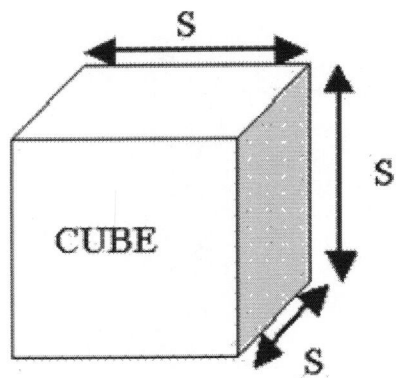

While the volume of a cylinder is equal to **πr²h**

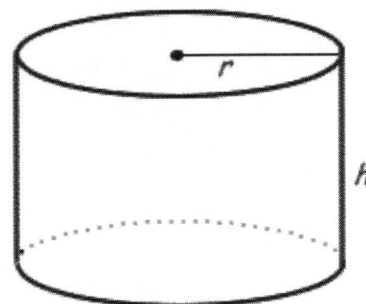

This maths is simple enough but clearly the way in which we use this information to solve problems is going to be the key. Let's look at a sample problem:

> If the length, width, and height of a rectangular box measures 1, 3, and 8, respectively, what is the total surface area of the box?
>
> A. 24
> B. 35
> C. 70
> D. 72
> E. 144
>
> To solve these questions we have to do the following:
>
> **Step 1: Read the question**
>
> Many candidates make the mistake of skimming the question. This strategy has worked well for them at A-Level and GCSE simply because these exams consistently provide information and then ask repetitive questions involving that information.
>
> A number of candidates looked at the data, picked answer A and are feeling good. But look back at the question; this question is about total surface area not volume.
>
> **Step 2: Turn the words into numbers**

If you thought your ability to read critically could be left behind having completed all the verbal reasoning questions then you are mistaken. Most of the maths problems in the TSA require a conversion of the words into numbers. This will make it easier to solve the problem and will help you to avoid falling into the traps which the TSA likes to present.

For this question, a simple sketch is likely to be very effective:

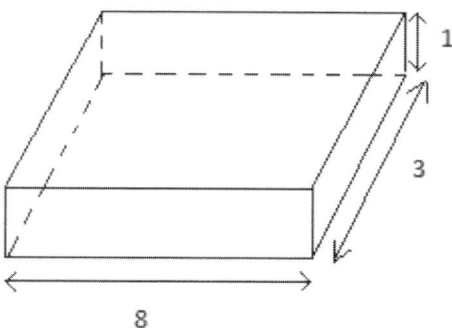

Step 3: Solve the question

This is the easy part!

There are 6 faces to a rectangle in total: Two faces with area 8x1 = 16
Two faces with area 3x1 = 6
Two faces with area 8x3 = 48

So the total area is simply 16 + 6 + 48 = 70

Therefore Answer C is correct.

Unfortunately all the TSA questions require careful thought in order to consistently get correct answers – this exam will require more concentration than almost anything else you've ever done in your life.

I make 18 cardboard cut-outs, each one from a piece of cardboard measuring 12cm x 10cm. Each cut out looks like this:

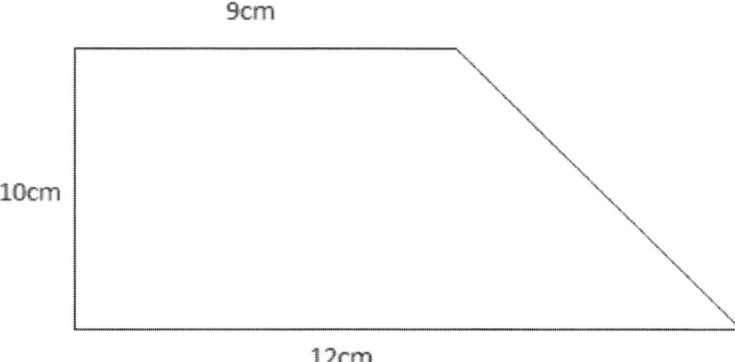

What is the total area of excess cardboard left over?

A. 150cm²
B. 270cm²
C. 540cm²
D. 360cm²
E. 105cm²

Step One: Read the question

This question wants you to make the mistake of calculating the area of the shape presented. If you do this, you'll get to answer E and you will have lost an easy mark.

Step Two: Turn the words into numbers

This question is about the shape which the question does not present, the left over cardboard. Leftover from what? The 12cm x 10cm rectangle that the shape presented has been cut from.

If we draw in this original shape it will help us to solve this question:

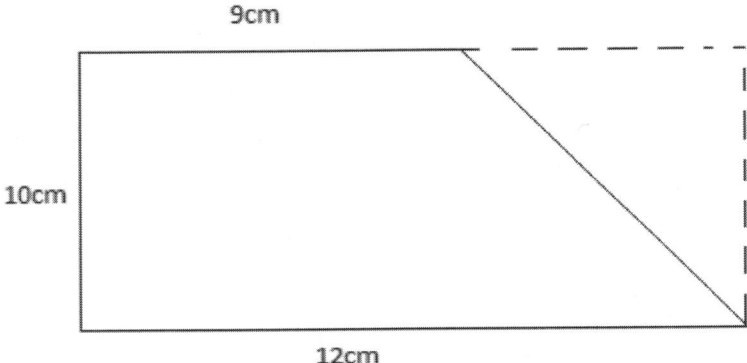

Step 3: Solve the question

Now we can see that the piece which was cut is an inverted triangle with a base of 3cm and a height of 10cm. The area of this triangle is 15cm². Since we have cut 18 pieces it means we now need to do 18 x 15 to get the final answer.

We could do long multiplication to get the answer and this will work but it will also take up valuable time. Instead we could see the following:

(15 x 20) – (15 x 2) = (15 x 18)

300 – 30 = 270 (answer choice B)

Multiplying 15 by 20 is an easy calculation we can do in our heads, as is 15 multiplied by 2. When we subtract the product of the latter from the former, we are left with the answer we want. It is little things like this which save us crucial seconds in the TSA. We must work quickly but accurately in these easier questions to ensure we have sufficient time for the more difficult questions.

Fractions

We will quickly remind ourselves the four key operations that we will need to perform with fractions:

Addition: In order to add fractions together, each fraction must have a common denominator. Following this simply add the numerators together.

Subtraction: Same as above but subtract one numerator from the other

Multiplication: Simply multiply the two numerators together and multiply the two denominators

Division: Flip the second fraction upside down and then multiply the first term by this inverted second term.

The TSA will never simply ask you to compute the result of two fractions. It will hide these fractions within some text. Let's look at an example:

A batch of cookies was divided among three tins: 2/3 of all the cookies were placed in either the blue tin or the green tin, and the rest were placed in the red tin. If 1/4 of all the cookies were placed in the blue tin, what fraction of the cookies that were placed in the other tins were placed in the green tin?

A. 15/2
B. 9/4
C. 5/9
D. 7/5
E. 9/7

Step One: Read the question

There is a lot of information in this text. We need to make sure we don't miss anything. One critical word missed is going to lead us to a trap answer. "other" – this question wants to know what fraction of the cookies are in the green tin from all the cookies in either the red or green tins. The question wants you to ignore the blue tin completely.

Step Two: Turn the words in numbers

Let's just set out what the paragraph tells us:

2/3 = Blue or Green

1/3 = Red

1/4 = Blue

From this we can work out that the green tin must have 5/12 of all the cookies:

1/4 + Green Cookies = 2/3

Therefore green cookies is equal to 5/12

Step Three: Pick numbers

At this point, we are at the stage where we have most of the information we need; namely the fraction of all the cookies in the green tin and the fraction of all the cookies in the red tin. However, working out (5/12)/((5/12)+(1/3)) would be quite tricky and time consuming.

Here it would be far easier to simply pick numbers. What we mean by this is, if you set the total number of cookies in the original problem at, say 12, you can then say the following:

There are: 4 red cookies
5 green cookies
3 blue cookies

Now you know you want the number of green cookies as a fraction of the number of green and red cookies, it is easy to see this is simply 5/9 – which matches answer choice C.

Picking numbers is an invaluable strategy which often cuts through lots of complicated maths. When picking numbers on a question like this – be sure to pick a number which is a common multiple of all the other numbers you are dealing with. Here we were dealing with thirds, quarters and twelfths. It is easy to see quickly that 12 is a common multiple of all three fractions which will make our maths later on in the question easy.

Let's focus on another example and see another strategy we can use for TSA questions:

For which of the following values of n is $\dfrac{20-n}{n}$ not an integer?

A. 1
B. 2
C. 3
D. 4
E. 5

Step One: Read the question

This question looks a bit scary, there's a fraction in it and there is some phrasing which makes us feel like the answer is not going to be obvious at all. Don't miss the word "Not". This word tells us that four answers will make the fraction above yield an integer, missing this word would likely lead us into a trap answer.

The important thing to realise is that this test is multiple choice! They have presented five potential answers, one of which is definitely correct. We will use the answers they have provided to guide our solution.

Step Two: Simplify the question:

Sometimes questions involving fractions can be simplified. Can you see what can be done with this question?

(20-n)/n can be split into two fractions; 20/n – n/n. But we know n/n is an integer, and we also know that if we subtract one integer from another, we will simply end up with another integer. So now we can totally ignore this.

Thus, this question really wants to know, for which of the five answers below is 20/n not an integer?

Step Three: Answer the question

Hopefully your mental arithmetic skills allow you to easily pick the answer out, but if they don't then test the answer choices until you find that C is the correct answer.

In this second question we have tried to break the question down into its most simple form to determine the answer as quickly as possible. Another option would have been to plug in each of the answer choices to the original fraction until we found an answer. This method, while lacking in subtlety and time efficiency would also lead us to the correct answer.

Percentage/Ratios

"Per Cent" simply means "of 100" and that's precisely what percentages are trying to tell us. What amount "of 100" does something represent.

TSA questions are designed to be tricky and challenging and will test your ability not just to understand percentages but also to interpret changes.

Let's remember that to determine what percentage, for example, of X goes into Y we could perform the following calculation:

$$(x/y) \times 100$$

I've also put ratios in this topic but they are not dissimilar from percentages, particularly in the way that the TSA expects you to manipulate information to determine the answer. Also remember that if the ratio of x:y in a solution is 2:3, then the percentage of the solution which is x is simply:

$$(2/5) \times 100$$

This is because for every five total parts of the solution (i.e. 2+3), 2 parts are made up of x.

Let's look at some examples now to clarify:

Hockey is an 11-a-side game, but a team may consist of up to 16 players, with unlimited substitutions allowed throughout a match of 70 minutes duration.

Roger captains the Buccaneers hockey team. He has 16 players for today's match. He will play the whole match himself, as will the goalkeeper. He intends to rotate all the others in a such a way that each of them spends the same total amount of time on the pitch.

How much time should each player (except Roger and the goalkeeper) spend on the pitch during today's match?

A. 39 3/8 minutes
B. 45 minutes
C. 46 2/3 minutes
D. 48 1/8 minutes
E. 55 minutes

Step One: Read the question

This is another question with a lot of precise detail. We need to extract out the relevant information to make sure we answer the right question.

Step Two: Turn the words into numbers

The key here is that 14 players will be equally rotated around 9 positions for 70 minutes. This means that each player will only be able to play for 9/14th of the 70minutes.

We can now calculate the answer.

> Try to complete the maths yourself – it will be a good chance to practice cross multiplying fractions.

Let's now look at another example which is slightly more complicated:

> In what ratio should a 20% methyl alcohol solution be mixed with a 50% methyl alcohol solution so that the resultant solution has 40% methyl alcohol in it?
>
> A. 1 : 2
> B. 2 : 1
> C. 1 : 3
> D. 3 : 1
> E. 2 : 3

Step One: Read the question

This is a question where every answer except for the correct one is a trap! It is designed to punish those that fail to read the question carefully. We have to mix a 20% methyl solution with a 50% methyl solution in such a way that we end up with a 40% methyl solution

Let's just make a quick picture to make life easier:

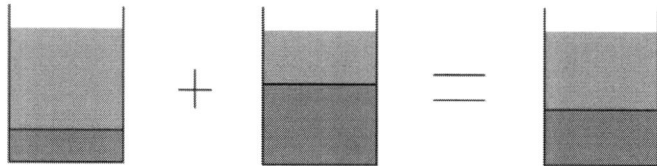

Step Two: Apply some logic

We know that we have to mix these solutions to end up with something that contains 40% methyl alcohol. We know that 50% is greater than 40%, while 20% is less than 40%. Thus we need to effectively use the 20% solution to dilute the 50% solution. This can be the starting point to work out the answer.

Step Three: Use the answer choices to guide your work

We will go through a mathematical solution for this later, but first let's see if we could use the answer choices to our advantage. We can see that there are effectively just three answer choices: 1:2, 1:3 or 2:3. We could use this knowledge to pick numbers and see what happens. Let's start logically with the first answer choice:

If we assume we had 100ml of the 50% solution, then we know we have 50ml of methyl alcohol in it. Combined with 50ml of the 20% solution, that's another 10ml of methyl alcohol.

So now we have a 150ml solution which contains 60ml of methyl alcohol. That cancels down as a fraction to 2/5 which is 40% and is indeed the answer.

Do you see how instead of using a lot of maths, this method let us take advantage of the TSA and the fact that it presents answer choices for us?

Alternate Step Three: Maths

> Let there be 1 litre of the solution after mixing 20% methyl alcohol and 50% methyl alcohol..
>
> If the concentration of methyl alcohol in it is 40%, then 0.4 litres of the resultant mixture is methyl alcohol.
>
> Let x litres of the solution containing 20% methyl alcohol be mixed with (1 - x) litres of the solution containing 50% methyl alcohol to get 1 litre of the solution containing 40% methyl alcohol.
>
> X litres of 20% methyl alcohol solution will contain 20% of x = 0.2x litres of methyl alcohol in it.
>
> (1 - x) litres of 50% methyl alcohol solution will contain 50% of (1- x) = 0.5(1 - x) litres of methyl alcohol.
>
> The sum of these quantities of methyl alcohols added up to the total of 0.4 litres in the resultant mixture.
>
> Therefore, 0.2x + 0.5(1 - x) = 0.4 litres
> 0.2x + 0.5 - 0.5x = 0.4
> 0.5 - 0.4 = 0.5x - 0.2x
>
> x = $\frac{0.1}{0.3} = \frac{1}{3}$ litres
>
> And 1 - x = 1 - $\frac{1}{3} = \frac{2}{3}$ litres.
>
> So, the two solutions are mixed in the ratio of 1 : 2

Most importantly, do you see how using maths to find the solution would take a long time? We could have tested two of the possible answers in the time it took to do this maths, and there is less chance with our previous method that something goes slightly wrong.

Probability

Let's have a brief reminder of how probability theory works:

The probability of two events both happening is equal to P(A) x P(B)

The probability that one or the other occurs is: P(A) + P(B)

The total probability of all eventualities is always equal to 1. So the probability that neither A nor B occurs is simply: 1 – [P(A) + P(B)].

Let's look at some examples of probability questions that the TSA might ask:

Each time I break in a game of pool there is a chance that a ball will go in a pocket. A ball will go in a pocket once out of every three breaks. If I take three consecutive breaks, what is the probability that I will pot a ball at least once?

A. 1/27
B. 1/3
C. 1/9
D. 8/27
E. 19/27

Step one: Read the question

This question is asking us to compute the probability that we pot a ball at least once. That means there are three scenarios we are interested in:

1. We pot on one of the three breaks
2. We pot on two of the three breaks
3. We pot on all three of the breaks

Is this already feels like a lot of calculation for a question which ought to take us 1 minute and 48 seconds or less?

Step two: Use logic to determine the quickest route to an answer

This sort of question opens the door to making lots of mistakes in the calculation step so ideally we want to reduce the calculations. Let's think about all the iterations when I break in a game of pool

1	2	3
Pot	No Pot	No Pot
No Pot	**Pot**	No Pot
No Pot	No Pot	**Pot**
Pot	**Pot**	No Pot
Pot	No Pot	**Pot**
No Pot	**Pot**	**Pot**
No Pot	No Pot	No Pot

I have put all the scenarios in the table above for each of the three breaks. Can you see that of the 7 outcomes, 6 involve potting a ball? This means that only one scenario doesn't involve potting a ball. We can thus conclude that since probabilities add up to 1, we could just determine 1 – P(no pots in three breaks) and say that this is the probability that at least one ball is pot.

This yields 1 – (2/3 x 2/3 x 2/3) = 19/27

Where 2/3 is the probability that no ball is pot from the break.

This matches answer choice E.

Let's look at a slightly more complicated example where logic will reward smart workers:

Bob has a 10-sided die whose sides are labelled with the first 10 positive odd integers. What is the probability that the product of two rolls will equal 15?

A. 1/100
B. 1/50
C. 1/25
D. 3/20
E. 1/5

Step One: Read the question

This is precisely the sort of question where reading it very carefully is essential for success in the TSA. There is a lot of detail here and it needs to be dissected and understood in order for us to come to the correct answer.

Our 10-sided die in this problem is numbered with the first 10 positive ODD integers. Missing the word odd would lead us instantly into an incorrect answer. This die is numbered; 1, 3, 5, 7, 9, 11, 13, 15, 17, 19.

Had you not read the question properly you may have thought that only rolls of 5 (or 3) then 3 (or 5) would work and been lead to answer A which is incorrect.

Step Two: Consider the successful outcomes versus total outcomes

For probability questions it can be easy to make small errors which lead to wrong answers. Instead we can focus instead of the total number of outcomes possible, then consider all the times that we get successful outcomes. In this case, success occurs when two rolls lead to a product of 15.

So we are going to roll a 10 sided die twice, how many total outcomes are possible?

Of these outcomes, how many ways can we end up with a product of 15?

There are 100 possible outcomes, but only 4 are successful. The successes occur when we roll 1 and then 15, or 15 and then 1, or 3 and then 5, or 5 and then 3.

Be careful not to miss out on the fact that you could roll the 5 either first or second. Failure to do so leads you into trap answer B when in fact the answer is C; 4/100 = 1/25

Speed/Distance/Time

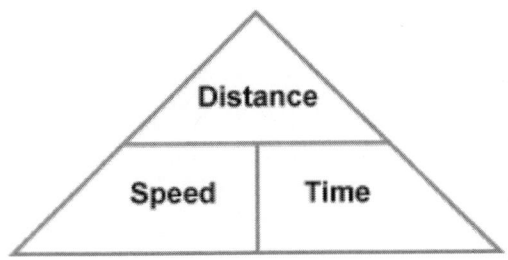

Some TSA questions involve speeds, distances and time. Let's all refresh our memories and remember that;

Distance = Speed x Time

Speed = Distance/Time

Time = Distance/Speed

With that, let's look at some past TSA questions to see how they expect you use this knowledge to solve problems:

> Andy lives at the bottom of a steep hill. The post office is at the top. Every Thursday he must walk up the hill to collect his pension. He manages to walk at 2 km per hour uphill and then 4km per hour downhill on the way back. The round trip, excluding the wait at the post office, takes him 4.5hours.
>
> How far is it from the house to the post office?
>
> A.   3km
> B.   6km
> C.   6.75km
> D.   12km
> E.   13.5km
>
> **Step One: Read the question**
>
> This question is all about the details. We need to make careful note of the speeds and the time taken for the entire journey. We should also be acutely aware of what this question wants us to determine.
>
> **Step Two: Using logic**
>
> Many of you will be tempted to compute the average speed (3km) and multiply it by the time of the entire experience. Can you work out why this is wrong? Andy does not walk at an average speed of 3km/hr because he spends more time going uphill than coming down.
>
> So we know that this information won't help us to solve this problem. However, we can logically deduce that because Andy walks uphill at half the speed he walks downhill, it is safe to assume he uses twice the amount of time to go uphill as he does to go back downhill.

Looking at the times, this means he must spend 3 hours going uphill and only 1.5 hours going back downhill. Now we can calculate the answer

Step Three: Avoid the final trap!

If you've read the question carefully, you should avoid the trap. Some of you will have no simply calculated that 3km per hour, walked for 2 hours means the journey uphill is 6km. Thus you've concluded that the total journey is 12km so answer D is correct. Right? Wrong! This question asked for the distance from the house to the post office, not the total distance Andy travelled.

Let's now think about a very common problem that the TSA will present; dealing with two different objects moving at different speeds:

Tessa sets off from Point A on her bike travelling at 20mph. Matt sets off from the same point at the same time following the same route in his car, travelling at 40mph. After 30 minutes, Matt realises that he has forgotten something behind at Point A and turns back to go and get it. He takes 15 minutes to gather his belongings then sets off again on the route, this time travelling at 50mph. At the same time that Matt sets off, Tessa stops for a long break.

How long after Matt sets off again will he pass Tessa?

- A. 30 minutes
- B. 15 minutes
- C. 60 minutes
- D. 20 minutes
- E. 45 minutes

Step one: Read the question

This question deals with two moving objects. It's important to consider each one separately. Tessa moves constantly at 20mph until she takes her break. Matt initially moves at 40mph but then must go back (it is not stated but we assume at 40mph also) and after 15minutes of no movement he then sets off at 50mph.

This question wants us to determine how long it takes Matt to overtake Tessa once he leaves the house for the second time.

Step Two: Process the information

Let's first calculate how long Tessa has travelled for. We can only do this using Matt's distances and speeds.

Matt initially travels for 30minutes, then he turns around and goes back which takes another 30minutes. He spends 15minutes stationary until he sets off again. At this point Tessa stops riding.

So Tessa has travelled for 75minutes at a constant 20mph. This implies she has travelled 25miles when Matt sets off again. Now we know that Matt will travel at 50mph until he has travelling 25miles, so the answer is simply A. 30 minutes.

Data in tables/graphs

The TSA sometimes presents data in graphs and tables and expects candidates to draw conclusions from the data available.

One of the most important skills to complete these questions successfully is to look at the axes and to understand what a change in the graph or table represents.

Let's look at this past TSA question and see how the question is designed to lead students into trap answers:

The graph above shows Northern Ireland house prices as a percentage of the UK average from the period 1988-2000.

What one of the following pieces of information can be inferred from the graph above?

(a) House prices in Northern Ireland fell by around 30% in the period shown
(b) House prices in Northern Ireland rose in some years and fell in others
(c) Average house prices in the UK (outside Northern Ireland) have risen over the period shown
(d) In some years average prices in North Ireland rose compared to those in the UK as a whole
(e) House prices in North Ireland peaked in 1988

Step One: Read the question

This question is about inference. Sometimes, inference questions will present you with answers which could be true, but which aren't absolutely true based on the information given. It is important to not fall into the trap of picking an answer which is possibly, or even probably correct. Instead, focus on choosing the answer which is definitely and indisputably true.

Step Two: Analyse the graph

Failure to take this step very seriously will result in lost marks on test day. It is essential to fully understand what the graph is showing us. In this instance, the graph is showing us house prices in Northern Ireland relative to the rest of the UK. So if house prices in northern Ireland are becoming relative less expensive compared to the UK as a whole, it does not mean that house prices in

Northern Ireland are falling. It may be that they are rising but at a slower rate. This is why understanding the data is essential.

Step Three: Evaluate the answer choices

Much as we did in the critical reasoning section of this document, we must now look at the answer choices and determine whether they can be inferred from the data above.

(a) This is a trap answer for those who fail to read the question properly. The graph isn't showing house prices in Northern Ireland, it is showing the relative value of a Northern Ireland house compared with the UK as a whole
(b) This might be true, and in fact is very likely to be true but we can't determine this from the information above
(c) Once again, this might be true but the graph isn't showing us information which confirms or refutes this point. Therefore it is out of scope and incorrect
(d) This is precisely what the data is getting across. If the average house price in Northern Ireland rose compared to the UK as a whole then you would expect the graph to slope upwards, which is does at certain points. If the average house price in Northern Ireland fell compared to the UK as a whole then you would expect the graph to trend downwards. We can see both of these on the graph above
(e) Picking this answer would again reveal a failure to understand what the graph is actually showing you and is incorrect

Let's now look at a table of information and see how we get on:

In a pie eating contest, 12 participants were given 30 minutes to eat as many pies as possible. A table showing their performance is given below:

Contestant	Pies Eaten
Anthony	19
Belinda	21
Carl	35
Didier	17
Eduardo	19
Fred	22
Gail	53
Hanna	12
Iain	46
Jeremy	44
Kyle	43
Linda	45

As a percentage, how many people ate between 21 and 40 pies?

A. 15%
B. 25%
C. 35%
D. 45%
E. 75%

Step One: Read the question

This question clearly wants you to pick out information from the table and to process it. The key here is to not waste time searching for information which is available in the text. Reading actively will help you avoid this error.

Step Two: Analyse the table

The helpful thing about the TSA is that you can write on the paper. At this point I would circle or tick the data which is relevant to this answer. I don't need to count the total number of people because the question stem has already told me that 12 people were competing in total. I've just saved a valuable 6 seconds!

We see that 3 out of 12 people ate between 21 and 40 pies, so the answer is B. 25%

Shapes/Spaces

Sometimes the TSA will ask questions related to shapes or space. The key here is to try and visualise the shape in question, or sometimes to try and pick a reference point on the shape in order to evaluate the question.

Let's start off by looking at an example in which a reference point can help to solve the problem:

Boland City has just installed a new tram system. Several artists have been asked to come up with a map of the system which, whilst it may not show the exact relative positions of the stations, shows the connections between them correctly.

The five maps are shown below (the names of the stations are not marked)

Four of the artists drew possible maps, but the fifth got the connections wrong. Which map below is based on incorrect connections?

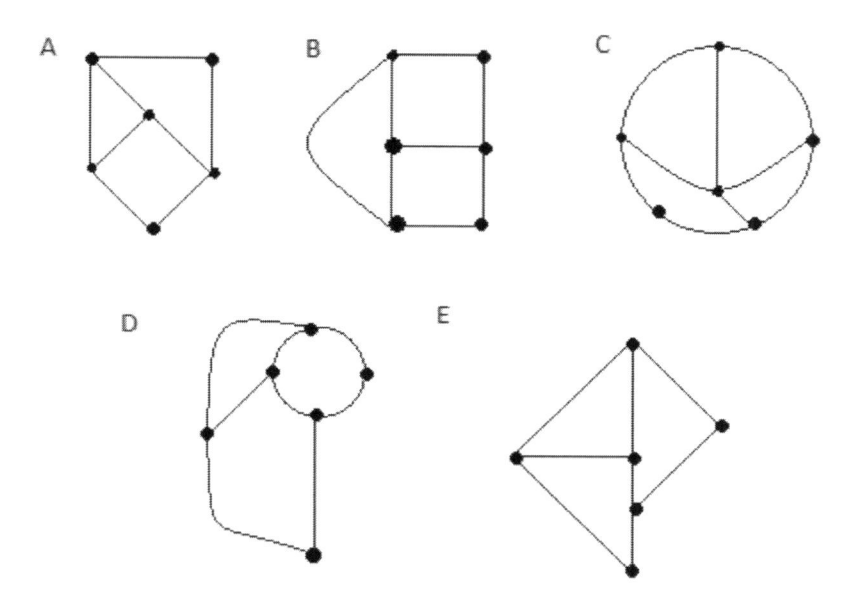

Step One: Read the question

Each of these pictures represents a tram map. While the positions of the stations might not be correct, the connections between the stations must be correct.

Step Two: Strategy 1

The first possible strategy you could use to solve such a question is to work on reference points.

First of all you can check something simple like making sure that the same number of stations are on the border of each diagram. (In this case, each map has 5 stations on the border). Had one of the diagrams had a different number on the outer edge it would have revealed the answer

Next you can focus on a new reference point, for example picking the central station. In four cases the central station is connected to three train stations but in one case (C) it is actually connected to four stations. This is very likely the answer we are looking for.

Step Two: Strategy 2

Instead of the strategy suggested above, another alternative would be to label the stations A-F. This is challenging and more time consuming because it also requires candidates to map very carefully how they label each diagram.

Once the diagrams are drawn, you can simply look for the odd one out, station by station. For example, if A was the station in the top left corner, you would ensure A was connected to the same stations in every map. You could keep doing this until you found one map in which one station was connected differently compared with all the others.

Let's look at another tricky example with some very tempting trap answers

The diagram shows the outline of a window which is intended to be composed of a number of panes of glass, all of the same size and shape.

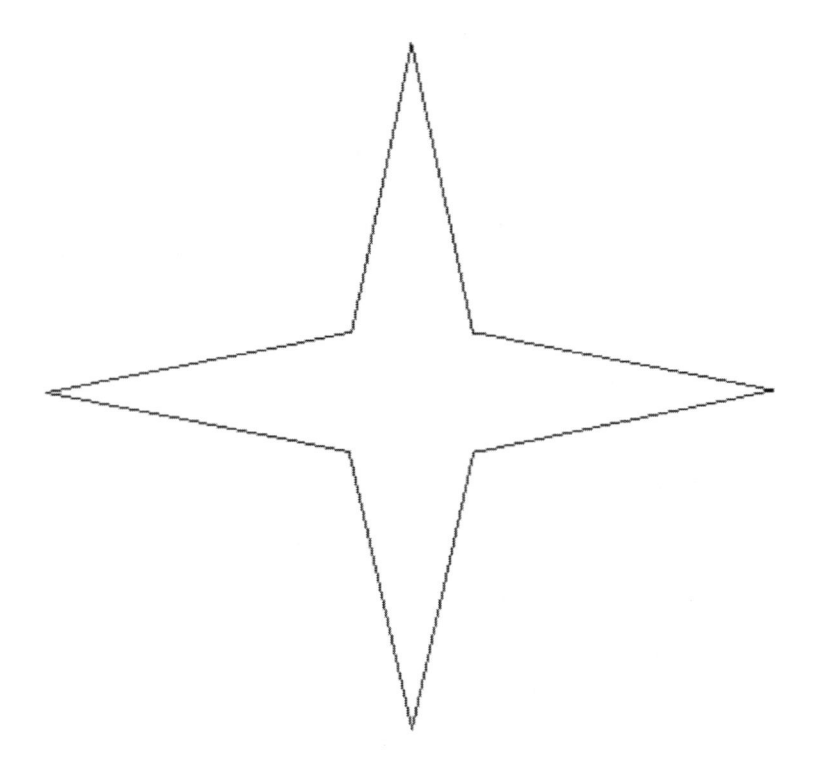

Which one of the shapes below could be used to fill this window?

A.

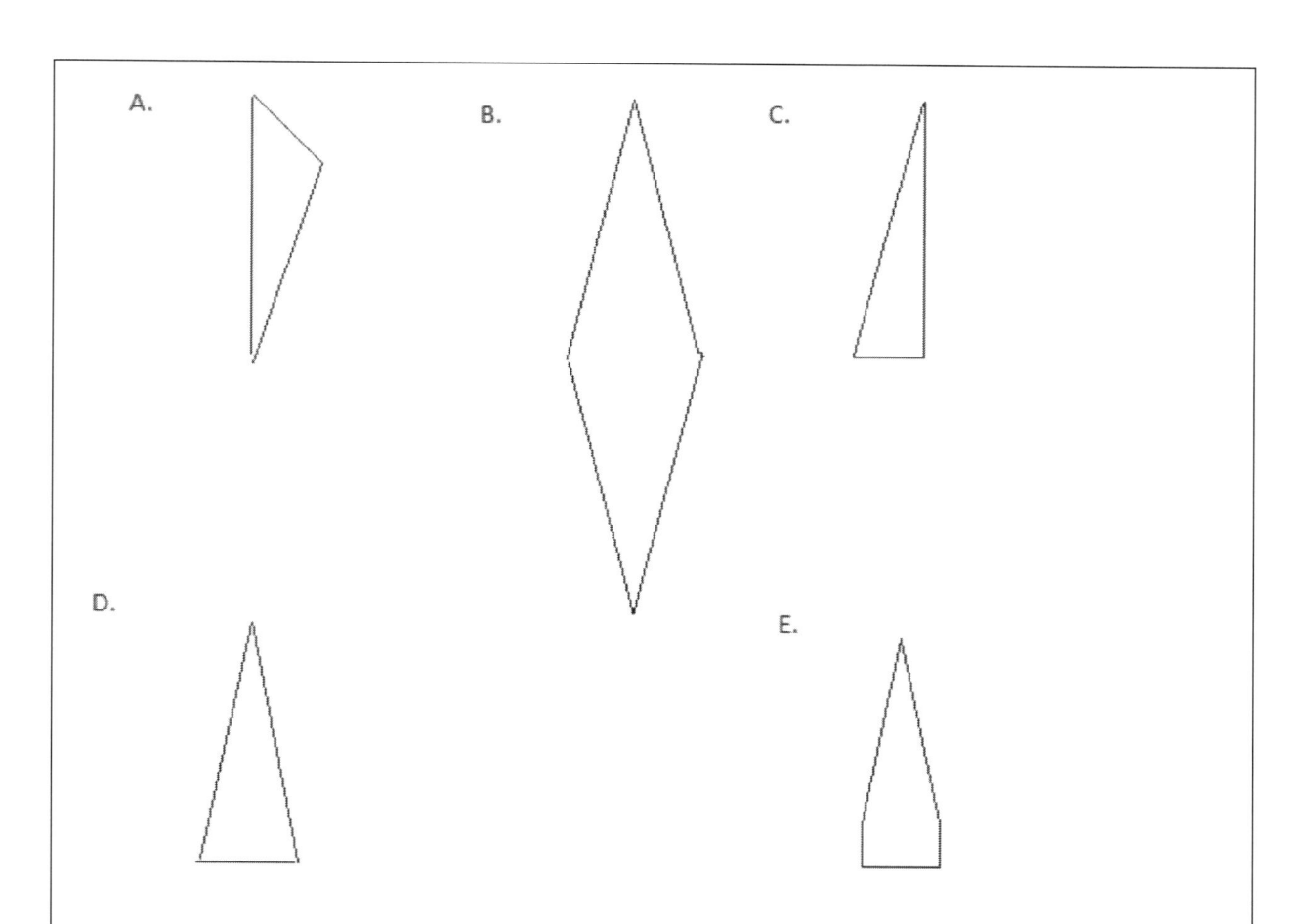

B.

C.

D.

E.

Step One: Read the question

All this question wants from us is to determine which shape will fit the space appropriately. Although it is not stated explicitly, when we scan the answer choices it may become clear that we want to select an answer which results in no overlap

Step Two: "Knock-out" answers

Rather than looking for the right answer let's start by working out which answers definitely won't work.

(e) Will result in overlap in the middle. Let's rule this out
(d) Won't properly fill in the centre. It is wrong.
(c) Also won't fill in the center
(b) Will overlap through the centre

So we have narrowed this question down to answer (a). When we look at shape a, it would definitely require 8 of them to perfectly fit the space with no overlap at all.

Take a look at these practice questions and see how you get on:

Which one of the four shapes matches the image of the cube folded up?

Choose the mirror image of the shape.

Which of the four possible options represent the cube shown from a different perspective?

Which one of these four shapes could be formed by putting the three shapes to the left together?

Practice Questions – Numerical

1. A project scheduled to be carried out over a single fiscal year has a budget of $12,600, divided into 12 equal monthly allocations. At the end of the fourth month of that fiscal year, the total amount actually spent on the project was $4,580. By how much was the project over its budget?

    A. $ 380
    B. $ 540
    C. $ 1,050
    D. $ 1,380
    E. $ 1,430

2. If the sum of 5, 8, 12 and 15 is equal to the sum of 3, 4, x + 3, what is the value of x?

    A. 14
    B. 15
    C. 16
    D. 17
    E. 18

3. For which of the following values of n is $\frac{100+n}{n}$ NOT an integer?

    A. 1
    B. 2
    C. 3
    D. 4
    E. 5

4. Rectangular Floors X and Y have equal area. If floor X is 12 feet by 18 feet and Floor Y is 9 feet wide, what is the length of Floor Y, in feet?

    A. 13½
    B. 18
    C. 18¾
    D. 21
    E. 24

| PAYROLL AT COMPANY X ||
No. of Employees	Salary
5	$20,000
4	$22,000
8	$25,000
3	$30,000

5. The table above shows the number of employees at each of four salary levels at Company X. What is the average (arithmetic mean) salary for the 20 employees?

   A. $23,500
   B. $23,750
   C. $23,900
   D. $24,125
   E. $24,250

6. A case contains c cartons. Each carton contains b boxes, and each box contains 100 paper clips. How many paper clips are contained in 2 cases?

   A. $100bc$
   B. $\dfrac{100b}{c}$
   C. $200bc$
   D. $\dfrac{200b}{c}$
   E. $\dfrac{200}{bc}$

7. A rainstorm increased the amount of water stored in State J reservoirs from 124 billion gallons to 138 billion gallons. If the storm increased the amount of water in the reservoirs to 82 percent of total capacity, approximately how many billion gallons of water were the reservoirs short of total capacity prior to the storm?

   A. 9
   B. 14
   C. 25
   D. 30
   E. 44

8. When $\dfrac{1}{10}$ percent of 5,000 is subtracted from $\dfrac{1}{10}$ of 5,000, the difference is

   A. 0
   B. 50
   C. 450
   D. 495
   E. 500

9. When Leo imported a certain item, he paid a 7 percent import tax on the portion of the total value of the item in excess of $1,000. If the amount of the import tax that Leo paid was $87.50, what was the total value of the item?

   A. $1,600
   B. $1,850

C. $2,250
D. $2,400
E. $2,750

10. On Monday, a person mailed 8 packages weighing an average (arithmetic mean) of $12\frac{3}{8}$ pounds, and on Tuesday, 4 packages weighing an average of $15\frac{1}{4}$ pounds. What was the average weight, in pounds, of all the packages the person mailed on both days?

- A. $13\frac{1}{3}$
- B. $13\frac{13}{16}$
- C. $15\frac{1}{2}$
- D. $15\frac{15}{16}$
- E. $16\frac{1}{2}$

11. $0.1 + (0.1)^2 + (0.1)^3 =$

- A. 0.1
- B. 0.111
- C. 0.1211
- D. 0.2341
- E. 0.3

12. A carpenter constructed a rectangular sandbox with a capacity of 10 cubic feet. If the carpenter were to make a similar sandbox twice as long, twice as wide, and twice as high as the first sandbox, what would be the capacity, in cubic feet, of the second sandbox?

- A. 20
- B. 40
- C. 60
- D. 80
- E. 100

13. A bakery opened yesterday with its daily supply of 40 dozen rolls. Half of the rolls were sold by noon and 80 percent of the remaining rolls were sold between noon and closing time. How many dozen rolls had not been sold when the bakery closed yesterday?

- A. 1
- B. 2
- C. 3
- D. 4
- E. 5

14. The ratio 2 to $\frac{1}{3}$ is equal to the ratio

   A. 6 to 1
   B. 5 to 1
   C. 3 to 2
   D. 2 to 3
   E. 1 to 6

15. If n is a prime number greater than 3, what is the remainder when n^2 is divided by 12?

   A. 0
   B. 1
   C. 2
   D. 3
   E. 5

16. $\dfrac{1}{1+1/3} - \dfrac{1}{1+1/2} =$

   A. $-\dfrac{1}{3}$
   B. $-\dfrac{1}{6}$
   C. $-\dfrac{1}{12}$
   D. $\dfrac{1}{12}$
   E. $\dfrac{1}{3}$

17. A rope 40 feet long is cut into two pieces. If one piece is 18 feet longer than the other, what is the length, in feet, of the shorter piece?

   A. 9
   B. 11
   C. 18
   D. 22
   E. 29

18. A student's average (arithmetic mean) test score on 4 tests is 78. What must be the student's score on a 5th test for the student's average score on the 5 tests to be 80?

   A. 80
   B. 82
   C. 84
   D. 86
   E. 88

19. How many minutes does it take John to type *y* words if he types at the rate of *x* words per minute?

    A. $\dfrac{x}{y}$

    B. $\dfrac{y}{x}$

    C. xy

    D. $\dfrac{60x}{y}$

    E. $\dfrac{y}{60x}$

20.

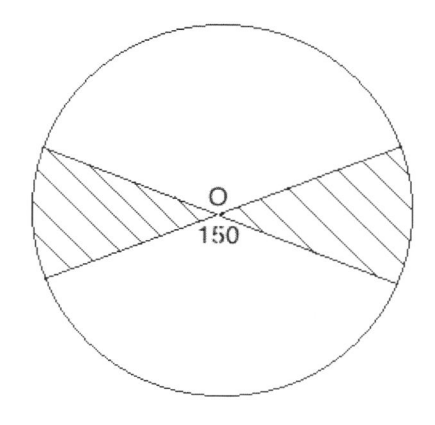

If *O* is the centre of the circle above, what fraction of the circular region is shaded?

    A. $\dfrac{1}{12}$

    B. $\dfrac{1}{9}$

    C. $\dfrac{1}{6}$

    D. $\dfrac{1}{4}$

    E. $\dfrac{1}{3}$

21. The sum $\dfrac{7}{8} + \dfrac{1}{9}$ is between

    A. $\dfrac{1}{2}$ and $\dfrac{3}{4}$

    B. $\dfrac{3}{4}$ and 1

    C. 1 and $1\dfrac{1}{4}$

    D. $1\dfrac{1}{4}$ and $1\dfrac{1}{2}$

    E. $1\dfrac{1}{2}$ and 2

22. $1 - (\dfrac{1}{2} - \dfrac{2}{3}) =$

A. $\frac{6}{5}$
B. $\frac{7}{6}$
C. $\frac{6}{7}$
D. $\frac{5}{6}$
E. 0

23. In a horticultural experiment, 200 seeds were planted in plot I and 300 were planted in plot II. If 57 percent of the seeds in plot I germinated and 42 percent of the seeds in plot II germinated, what percent of the total number of planted seeds germinated?

    A. 45.5%
    B. 46.5%
    C. 48.0%
    D. 49.5%
    E. 51.0%

24. In a certain population, there are 3 times as many people aged 21 or under as there are people over 21. The ratio of those 21 or under to the total population is

    A. 1 to 2
    B. 1 to 3
    C. 1 to 4
    D. 2 to 3
    E. 3 to 4

25. Kelly and Chris packed several boxes with books. If Chris packed 60 percent of the total number of boxes, what was the ratio of the number of boxes Kelly packed to the number of boxes Chris packed?

    A. 1 to 6
    B. 1 to 4
    C. 2 to 5
    D. 3 to 5
    E. 2 to 3

26. The average (arithmetic mean) of 10, 30, and 50 is 5 more than the average of 20, 40 and

    A. 15
    B. 25
    C. 35

D. 45
E. 55

27. A glucose solution contains 15 grams of glucose per 100 cubic centimetres of solution. If 45 cubic centimetres of the solution were poured into an empty container, how many grams of glucose would be in the container?

   A. 3.00
   B. 5.00
   C. 5.50
   D. 6.50
   E. 6.75

28. Lucy invested $10,000 in a new mutual fund account exactly three years ago. The value of the account increased by 10 percent during the first year, increased by 5 percent during the second year, and decreased by 10 percent during the third year. What is the value of the account today?

   A. $10,350
   B. $10,395
   C. $10,500
   D. $11,500
   E. $12,705

29. A certain fruit stand sold apples for $0.70 each and bananas for $0.50 each. If a customer purchased both apples and bananas from the stand for a total of $6.30, what total number of apples and bananas did the customer purchase?

   A. 10
   B. 11
   C. 12
   D. 13
   E. 14

30. At a certain school, the ratio of the number of second graders to the number of fourth graders is 8 to 5, and the ratio of the number of first graders to the number of second graders is 3 to 4. If the ratio of the number of third graders to the number of fourth graders is 3 to 2, what is the ratio of the number of first graders to the number of third graders?

   A. 16 to 15
   B. 9 to 5
   C. 5 to 16
   D. 5 to 4
   E. 4 to 5

31. A gym class can be divided into 8 teams with an equal number of players on each team or into 12 teams with an equal number of players on each team. What is the lowest possible number of students in the class?

   A. 20
   B. 24
   C. 36
   D. 48
   E. 96

32. In the Johnsons' monthly budget, the dollar amounts allocated to household expenses, food, and miscellaneous items are in the ratio 5:2:1, respectively. If the total amount allocated these three categories is $1,800, what is the amount allocated to food?

   A. $900
   B. $720
   C. $675
   D. $450
   E. $225

33. There are 4 more women than men on Centerville's board of education. If there are 10 members on the board, how many are women?

   A. 3
   B. 4
   C. 6
   D. 7
   E. 8

| Amount of bacteria present ||
Time	Amount (grams)
1.00pm	10.0
4.00pm	X
7.00pm	14.4

34. Data for a certain biology experiment are given in the table above. If the amount of bacteria present increased by the same factor during each of the two 3-hour periods shown, how many grams of bacteria were present at 4:00PM?

   A. 12.0
   B. 12.1
   C. 12.2
   D. 12.3
   E. 12.4

35. A certain store sells all maps at one price and all books at another price. On Monday the store sold 12 maps and 10 books for a total of $38.00, and on Tuesday the store sold 20 maps and 15 books for a total of $60.00. At this store, how much less does a map sell for than a book?

   A. $0.25
   B. $0.50
   C. $0.75
   D. $1.00
   E. $1.25

36. A store reported total sales of $385 million for February of this year. If the total sale for the same month last year was $320 million, approximately what was the percent increase in sales?

   A. 2%
   B. 17%
   C. 20%
   D. 65%
   E. 83%

37. In a certain city, 60 percent of the registered voters are Democrats and the rest are Republicans. In a mayoral race, if 75% of the registered voters who are Democrats and 20% of the registered voters who are Republicans are expected to vote for candidate A, what percent of the registered voters are expected to vote for candidate A?

   A. 50%
   B. 53%
   C. 54%
   D. 55%
   E. 57%

38. Water consists of hydrogen and oxygen and the approximate ratio, by mass, of hydrogen to oxygen is 2:16. Approximately how many grams of Oxygen are there in 144 grams of water?

   A. 16
   B. 72
   C. 112
   D. 128
   E. 142

39. The present ratio of students to teachers at a certain school is 30 to 1. If the student enrolment were to increase by 50 students and the number of teachers were to increase by 5, the ratio of students to teachers would then be 25 to 1. What is the present number of teachers?

A. 5
B. 8
C. 10
D. 12
E. 15

40. Sixty percent of the members of a study group are women and 45 percent of those women are lawyers. If one member of the study group is to be selected at random, what is the probability that the member selected is a woman lawyer?

    A. 0.10
    B. 0.15
    C. 0.27
    D. 0.33
    E. 0.45

41. A pharmaceutical company received $3 million in royalties on the first $20 million in sales of the generic equivalent of one of its products and then $9 million in royalties on the next $108 million in sales. By approximately what percent did the ratio of royalties to sales decrease from the first $20 million in sales to the next $108 million in sales?

    A. 8%
    B. 15%
    C. 45%
    D. 52%
    E. 56%

42. If candy bars that regularly sell for $0.40 each are on sale at two for $0.75, what is the percent reduction in the price of two such candy bars purchased at the sale price?

    A. $2\frac{1}{2}\%$
    B. $6\frac{1}{4}\%$
    C. $6\frac{2}{3}\%$
    D. 8%
    E. $12\frac{1}{2}\%$

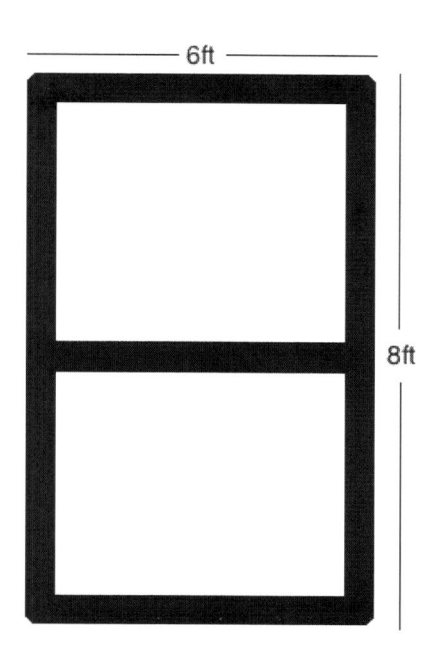

43. The front of a 6-foot-by-8-foot rectangular door has brass rectangular trim, as indicated by the shading in the figure above. If the trim is uniformly 1 foot wide, what fraction of the door's front surface is covered by the trim?

    A. $\frac{13}{48}$
    B. $\frac{5}{12}$
    C. $\frac{1}{2}$
    D. $\frac{7}{12}$
    E. $\frac{5}{8}$

44. Mary's income is 60 percent more than Tim's income, and Tim's income is 40 percent less than Juan's income. What percent of Juan's income is Mary's income

    A. 124%
    B. 120%
    C. 96%
    D. 80%
    E. 64%

45. On a recent trip, Cindy drove her care 290 miles, rounded to the nearest 10 miles, and used 12 gallons of gasoline, rounded to the nearest gallon. The actual number of miles per gallon that Cindy's car got on the trip must have been between

    A. $\frac{290}{12.5}$ and $\frac{290}{11.5}$
    B. $\frac{295}{12}$ and $\frac{285}{11.5}$
    C. $\frac{285}{12}$ and $\frac{295}{12}$

D. $\frac{285}{12.5}$ and $\frac{295}{11.5}$

E. $\frac{295}{12.5}$ and $\frac{285}{11.5}$

46. In a small snack shop, the average (arithmetic mean) revenue was $400 per day over a 10-day period. During this period, if the average daily revenue was $360 for the first 6 days, what was the average daily revenue for the last 4 days?

　　A. $420
　　B. $440
　　C. $450
　　D. $460
　　E. $480

47. At a loading dock, each worker on the night crew loaded ¾ as many boxes as each worker on the day crew. If the night crew has 4/5 as many workers as the day crew, what fraction of all the boxes loaded by the two crews did the day crew load?

　　A. 1/2
　　B. 2/5
　　C. 3/5
　　D. 4/5
　　E. 5/8

48. A restaurant meal cost $35.50 and there was no tax. If the tip was more than 10 percent but less than 15 percent of the cost of the meal, then the total amount paid must have been between

　　A. $40 and $42
　　B. $39 and $41
　　C. $38 and $40
　　D. $37 and $39
　　E. $36 and $37

49. A club collected exactly $599 from its members. If each member contributed at least $12, what is the greatest number of members the club could have?

　　A. 43
　　B. 44
　　C. 49
　　D. 50
　　E. 51

50. A toy store regularly sells all stock at a discount of 20 percent to 40 percent. If an additional 25 percent were deducted from the discount price during a special sale, what would be the lowest possible price of a toy costing $16 before any discount?

A. $5.60
B. $7.20
C. $8.80
D. $9.60
E. $15.20

51. Jack is now 14 years older than Bill. If in 10 years Jack will be twice as old as Bill, how old will Jack be in 5 years?

   A. 9
   B. 19
   C. 21
   D. 23
   E. 33

52. An empty pool being filled with water at a constant rate takes 8 hours to fill to 3/5 of its capacity. How much more time will it take to finish filling the pool?

   A. 5 hr 30 min
   B. 5 hr 20 min
   C. 4 hr 48 min
   D. 3 hr 12 min
   E. 2 hr 40 min

53. A tank contains 10,000 gallons of a solution that is 5 percent sodium chloride by volume. If 2,500 gallons of water evaporate from the tank, the remaining solution will be approximately what percent sodium chloride?

   A. 1.25%
   B. 3.75%
   C. 6.25%
   D. 6.67%
   E. 11.7%

54. A fruit-salad mixture consists of apples, peaches, and grapes in the ratio 6:5:2, respectively, by weight. If 39 pounds of the mixture is prepared, the mixture includes how many more pounds of apples than grapes?

   A. 15
   B. 12
   C. 9
   D. 6
   E. 4

55. During a certain season, a team won 80 percent of its first 100 games and 50 percent of its remaining games. If the team won 70 percent of its games for the entire season, what was the total number of games that the team played?

   A. 180
   B. 170
   C. 156
   D. 150
   E. 105

56. Last year, for every 100 million vehicles that travelled on a certain highway, 96 vehicles were involved in accidents. If 3 billion vehicles travelled on the highway last year, how many of those vehicles were involved in accidents? (1 billion = 1,000,000,000)

   A. 288
   B. 320
   C. 2,880
   D. 3,200
   E. 28,800

57. The probability is ½ that a certain coin will turn up heads on any given toss. If the coin is to be tossed three times, what is the probability that on at least one of the tosses the coin will turn up tails?

   A. 1/8
   B. 1/2
   C. 3/4
   D. 7/8
   E. 15/16

58. The ratio of two quantities is 3 to 4. If each of the quantities is increased by 5, what is the ratio of these two new quantities?

   A. 3/4
   B. 8/9
   C. 18/19
   D. 23/24
   E. It cannot be determined from the information given.

59. If ½ of the air in a tank is removed with each stroke of a vacuum pump, what fraction of the original amount of air has been removed after 4 strokes?

   A. 15/16
   B. 7/8
   C. 1/4

D. 1/8
E. 1/16

60. For the past *n* days, the average (arithmetic mean) daily production at a company was 50 units. If today's production of 90 units raises the average to 55 units per day, what is the value of n?

A. 30
B. 18
C. 10
D. 9
E. 7

61. A part-time employee whose hourly wage was increased by 25 percent decided to reduce the number of hours worked per week so that the employee's total weekly income would remain unchanged. By what percent should the number of hours worked be reduced?

A. 12.5%
B. 20%
C. 25%
D. 50%
E. 75%

62. If n is an integer, which of the following must be even?

A. n+1
B. n+2
C. 2n
D. 2n+1
E. n^2

63. A glass was filled with 10ml of water and 0.01ml evaporated each day during a 20 day period. What percent of the original amount of water evaporated during this period?

A. 0.002%
B. 0.02%
C. 0.2%
D. 2%
E. 20%

64. Machine A produces bolts at a uniform rate of 120 every 40 seconds and Machine B produces bolts at a uniform rate of 100 every 20 seconds. If the two machines run simultaneously, how many seconds will it take for them produce a total of 200 widgets?

A. 22

B. 25
C. 28
D. 32
E. 56

65. If n is an integer (whole number) greater than 6, which of the following must be divisible by 3?

    A. n(n+1)(n-4)
    B. n(n+2)(n-1)
    C. n(n+3)(n-5)
    D. n(n+4)(n-2)
    E. n(n+5)(n-6)

Practice Questions – Verbal

1. "Life expectancy" is the average age at death of the entire live-born population. In the middle of the nineteenth century, life expectancy in North America was 40 years, whereas now it is nearly 80 years. Thus, in those days, people must have been considered old at an age that we now consider the prime of life.

Which of the following, if true, undermines the argument above?

   A. In the middle of the nineteenth century, the population of North America was significantly smaller than it is today.
   B. Most of the gains in life expectancy in the last 150 years have come from reductions in the number of infants who die in their first year of life.
   C. Many of the people who live to an advanced age today do so only because of medical technology that was unknown in the nineteenth century.
   D. The proportion of people who die in their seventies is significantly smaller today than is the proportion of people who die in their eighties.
   E. More people in the middle of the nineteenth century engaged regularly in vigorous physical activity than do so today.

2. Homeowners aged 40 to 50 are more likely to purchase ice cream and are more likely to purchase it in larger amounts than are members of any other demographic group. The popular belief that teenagers eat more ice cream than adults must, therefore, be false.

The argument is flawed primarily because the author

   A. Fails to distinguish between purchasing and consuming.
   B. Does not supply information about homeowners in age groups other than 40 to 50.
   C. Depends on popular belief rather than on documented research findings.
   D. Does not specify the precise amount of ice cream purchased by any demographic group.
   E. Discusses ice cream rather than more nutritious and healthful foods.

3. According to a prediction of the not-so-distant future published in 1940, electricity would revolutionize agriculture. Electrodes would be inserted into the soil and the current between them would kill bugs and weeds and make crop plants stronger.

Which of the following, if true, most strongly indicates that the logic of the prediction above is flawed?

   A. In order for farmers to avoid electric shock while working in the fields, the current could be turned off at such times without diminishing the intended effects.

B. If the proposed plan for using electricity were put into practice, farmers would save on chemicals now being added to the soil.
C. It cannot be taken for granted that the use of electricity is always beneficial.
D. Since weeds are plants, electricity would affect weeds in the same way as it would affect crop plants.
E. Because a planting machine would need to avoid coming into contact with the electrodes, new parts for planting machines would need to be designed.

4. In order to reduce the number of items damaged while in transit to customers, packaging consultants recommended that the TrueSave mail-order company increase the amount of packing material so as to fill any empty spaces in its cartons. Accordingly, True~Save officials instructed the company's packers to use more packing material than before, and the packers zealously acted on these instructions and used as much as they could. Nevertheless, customer reports of damaged items rose somewhat.

Which of the following, if true, most helps to explain why acting on the consultants' recommendation failed to achieve its goal?

A. The change in packing policy led to an increase in expenditure on packing material and labour.
B. When packing material is compressed too densely, it loses some of its capacity to absorb shock.
C. The amount of packing material used in a carton does not significantly influence the ease with which a customer can unpack the package.
D. Most of the goods that True Save ships are electronic products that are highly vulnerable to being damaged in transit.
E. TrueSave has lost some of its regular customers as a result of the high number of damaged items they received.

5. Cable television spokesperson: Subscriptions to cable television are a bargain in comparison to "free" television is not really free. It is consumers, in the end, who pay for the costly advertising that supports "free" television.

Which of the following, if true, is most damaging to the position of the cable-television spokesperson?

A. Consumers who do not own television sets are less likely to be influenced in their purchasing decisions by television advertising than are consumers who own television sets.
B. Subscriptions to cable television include access to some public-television channels, which do not accept advertising.
C. For locations with poor television reception, cable television provides picture quality superior to that provided by free television.
D. There is as much advertising on many cable-television channels as there is on "free" television channels.

E. Cable-television subscribers can choose which channels they wish to receive.

6. Wood smoke contains dangerous toxins that cause changes in human cells. Because wood smoke presents such a high health risk, legislation is needed to regulate the use of open-air fires and wood-burning stoves.

Which of the following, if true, provides the most support for the argument above?

- A. The amount of dangerous toxins contained in wood smoke is much less than the amount contained in an equal volume of automobile exhaust.
- B. Within the jurisdiction covered by the proposed legislation, most heating and cooking is done with oil or natural gas.
- C. Smoke produced by coal-burning stoves is significantly more toxic than smoke from wood-burning stoves.
- D. No significant beneficial effect on air quality would result if open-air fires were banned within the jurisdiction covered by the proposed legislation.
- E. In valleys where wood is used as the primary heating fuel, the concentration of smoke results in poor air quality.

7. In Washington County, attendance at the movies is just large enough for the cinema operators to make modest profits. The size of the county's population is stable and is not expected to increase much. Yet there are investors ready to double the number of movie screens in the county within five years, and they are predicting solid profits both for themselves and for the established cinema operators.

Which of the following, if true about Washington County, most helps to provide a justification for the investors' prediction?

- A. Over the next ten years, people in their teenage years, the prime movie-going age, will be a rapidly growing proportion of the county's population.
- B. As distinct from the existing cinemas, most of the cinemas being planned would be located in downtown areas, in hopes of stimulating an economic revitalization of those areas.
- C. Spending on video purchases, as well as spending on video rentals, has been increasing modestly each year for the past ten years.
- D. The average number of screens per cinema is lower among existing cinemas than it is among cinemas still in the planning stages.
- E. The sale of snacks and drinks in cinemas accounts for a steadily growing share of most cinema operators' profits.

8. A conservation group in the United States is trying to change the long-standing image of bats as frightening creatures. The group contends that bats are feared and persecuted solely because they are shy animals that are active only at night.

Which of the following, if true, would cast the most serious doubt on the accuracy of the group's contention?

A. Bats are steadily losing natural roosting places such as caves and hollow trees and are thus turning to more developed areas for roosting.
B. Bats are the chief consumers of nocturnal insects and thus can help make their hunting territory more pleasant for humans.
C. Bats are regarded as frightening creatures not only in the United States but also in Europe, Africa and South America.
D. Raccoons and owls are shy and active only at night, yet they are not generally feared and persecuted.
E. People know more about the behaviour of other greatly feared animal species, such as lions, alligators and snakes, than they do about the behaviour of bats.

9. Hunter: **Many people blame hunters alone for the decline in Greenrock National Forest's deer population over the past ten years.** Yet clearly, black bears have also played an important role in this decline. In the past ten years, the forest's protected black bear population has risen sharply, and examination of black bears found dead in the forest during the deer hunting season showed that a number of them had recently fed on deer.

In the hunter's argument, the portion in boldface plays which of the following roles?

A. It is the main conclusion of the argument
B. It is a finding that the argument seeks to explain
C. It is an explanation that the argument concludes is correct
D. It provides evidence in support of the main conclusion of the argument
E. It introduces a judgement that the argument opposes.

10. In Asia, where palm trees are non-native, the trees' flowers have traditionally been pollinated by hand, which has kept palm fruit productivity unnaturally low. When weevils known to be efficient pollinators of palm flowers were introduced into Asia in 1980, palm fruit productivity increased – by up to 50 percent in some areas – but then decreased sharply in 1984.

Which of the following statements, if true, would best explain the 1984 decrease in productivity?

A. Prices for palm fruit fell between 1980 and 1984 following the rise in production and a concurrent fall in demand.
B. Imported trees are often more productive than native trees because the imported ones have left behind their pests and diseases in their native lands.
C. Rapid increases in productivity tend to deplete trees of nutrients needed for the development of the fruit-producing female flowers.
D. The weevil population in Asia remained at approximately the same level between 1980 and 1984.

E. Prior to 1980 another species of insect pollinated the Asian palm trees, but not as efficiently as the species of weevil that was introduced in 1980.

11. Physician: The hormone melatonin has shown promise as a medication for sleep disorders when taken in synthesized form. Because the long-term side effects of synthetic melatonin are unknown, however, I cannot recommend its use at this time.

Patient: Your position is inconsistent with your usual practice. You prescribe many medications that you know have serious side effects, so concern about side effects cannot be the real reason you will not prescribe melatonin.

The patient's argument is flawed because it fails to consider that

A. The side effects of synthetic melatonin might be different from those of naturally produced melatonin.
B. It is possible that the physician does not believe that melatonin has been conclusively shown to be effective.
C. Sleep disorders, if left untreated, might lead to serious medical complications.
D. The side effe4cts of a medication can take some time to manifest themselves.
E. Known risks can be weighed against known benefits, but unknown risks cannot.

12. Male bowerbirds construct elaborately decorated nests, or bowers. Basing their judgment on the fact that different local populations of bowerbirds of the same species build bowers that exhibit different building and decorative styles, researchers have concluded that the bowerbirds' building styles are a culturally acquired, rather than a genetically transmitted, trait.

Which of the following, if true, would most strengthen the conclusion drawn by the researchers?

A. There are more common characteristics than there are differences among the bower-building styles of the local bowerbird population that has been studied most extensively.
B. Young male bowerbirds are inept at bower-building and apparently spend years watching their elders before becoming accomplished in the local bower style.
C. The bowers of one species of bowerbird lack the towers and ornamentation characteristic of the bowers of most other species of bowerbird.
D. Bowerbirds are found only in New Guinea and Australia, where local populations of the birds apparently seldom have contact with one another.
E. It is well known that the song dialects of some songbirds are learned rather than transmitted genetically.

13. A drug that is highly effective in treating many types of infection can, at present, be obtained only from the bark of the ibora, a tree that is quite rare in the wild. It takes the

bark of 5,000 trees to make one kilogram of the drug must inevitably lead to the ibora's extinction.

Which of the following, if true, most seriously weakens the argument above?

- A. The drug made from ibora bark is dispensed to the doctors from a central authority.
- B. The drug made from ibora bark is expensive to produce.
- C. The leaves of the ibora are used in a number of medical products.
- D. The ibora can be propagated from cuttings and grown under cultivation.
- E. The ibora generally grows in largely inaccessible places.

14. Many breakfast cereals are fortified with vitamin supplements. Some of these cereals provide 100 percent of the recommended daily requirement of vitamins. Nevertheless, a well-balanced breakfast, including a variety of foods, is a better source of those vitamins than are such fortified breakfast cereals alone.

Which of the following, if true, would most strongly support the position above?

- A. In many foods, the natural combination of vitamins with other nutrients makes those vitamins more usable by the body than are vitamins added in vitamin supplements.
- B. People who regularly eat cereals fortified with vitamin supplements sometimes neglect to eat the foods in which the vitamins occur naturally.
- C. Foods often must be fortified with vitamin supplements because naturally occurring vitamins are removed during processing.
- D. Unprocessed cereals are naturally high in several of the vitamins that are usually added to fortified breakfast cereals.
- E. Cereals containing vitamin supplements are no harder to digest than similar cereals without added vitamins.

15. When a polygraph test is judged inconclusive, this is no reflection on the examinee. Rather, such a judgement means that the test has failed to show whether the examinee was truthful or untruthful. Nevertheless, employers will sometimes refuse to hire a job applicant because of an inconclusive polygraph test result.

Which of the following conclusions can most properly be drawn from the information above?

- A. Most examinees with inconclusive polygraph test results are in fact untruthful.
- B. Polygraph tests should not be used by employers in the consideration of job applicants.
- C. An inconclusive polygraph test result is sometimes unfairly held against the examinee.

D. A polygraph test indicating that an examinee is untruthful can sometimes be mistaken.
E. Some employers have refused to consider the results of polygraph tests when evaluating job applicants.

16. The technological conservatism of bicycle manufacturers is a reflection of the kinds of demand they are trying to meet. The only cyclists seriously interested in innovation and willing to pay for it are bicycle racers. Therefore, innovation in bicycle technology is limited by what authorities will accept as standard for purposes of competition in bicycle races.

Which of the following is an assumption made in drawing the conclusion above?

A. The market for cheap, traditional bicycles cannot expand unless the market for high-performance competition bicycles expands.
B. High performance bicycles are likely to be improved more as a result of technological innovations developed in small workshops than as a result of technological innovations developed in major manufacturing concerns.
C. Bicycle racers do not generate a strong demand for innovations that fall outside what is officially recognised as standard for purposes of competition.
D. The technological conservatism of bicycle manufacturers results primarily from their desire to manufacture a product that can be sold without being altered to suit different national markets.
E. The authorities who set standards for high-performance bicycle racing do not keep informed about innovative bicycle design.

17. A company's two divisions performed with remarkable consistency over the past three years: in each of those years, the pharmaceuticals division has accounted for roughly 20 percent of dollar sales and 40 percent of profits, and the chemicals division for the balance.

Which of the following can properly be inferred regarding the past three years from the statement above?

A. Total dollar sales for each of the company's divisions have remained roughly constant.
B. The pharmaceuticals division has faced stiffer competition in its markets than has the chemicals division.
C. The chemicals division has realized lower profits per dollar of sales than has the pharmaceuticals division.
D. The product mix offered by each of the company's divisions has remained unchanged.
E. Highly profitable products accounted for a higher percentage of the chemicals division's sales than those of the pharmaceuticals division's.

18. Which of the following most logically completes the argument?

Ferber's syndrome, a viral disease that frequently affects cattle, is transmitted to these animals through infected feed. Even though chickens commercially raised for meat are often fed the type of feed identified as the source of infection in cattle, Ferber's syndrome is only rarely observed in chickens. This fact, however, does not indicate that most chickens are immune to the virus that causes Ferber's syndrome, since ____

    A. Chickens and cattle are not the only kinds of farm animal that are typically fed the type of feed liable to be contaminated with the virus that causes Ferber' syndrome.
    B. Ferber's syndrome has been found in animals that have not been fed the type of feed liable to be contaminated with the virus that can cause the disease.
    C. Resistance to some infectious organisms such as the virus that causes Ferber's syndrome can be acquired by exposure to a closely related infectious organism.
    D. Chickens and cattle take more than a year to show symptoms of Ferber's syndrome, and chickens commercially raised to meat, unlike cattle, are generally brought to market during the first year of life.
    E. The type of feed liable to be infected with the virus that causes Ferber's syndrome generally constitutes a larger proportion of the diet of commercially raised chickens than of commercially raised cattle.

19. Last year the rate of inflation was 1.2 percent, but for the current year it has been 4 percent. We can conclude that inflation is on an upward trend and the rate will be still higher next year.

Which of the following, if true, most seriously weakens the conclusion above?

    A. The inflation figures were computed on the basis of a representative sample of economic data rather than all of the available data.
    B. Last year a dip in oil prices brought inflation temporarily below its recent stable annual level of 4 percent.
    C. Increases in the pay of some workers are tied to the level of inflation, and at an inflation rate of 4 percent or above, these pay rises constitute a force causing further inflation.
    D. The 1.2 percent rate of inflation last year represented a 10 year low.
    E. Government intervention cannot affect the rate of inflation to any significant degree.

20. Offshore oil-drilling operations entail an unavoidable risk of an oil spill, but importing oil on tankers presently entails an even greater such risk per barrel of oil. Therefore, if we are to reduce the risk of an oil spill without curtailing our use of oil, we must invest more in offshore operations and import less oil on tankers.

Which of the following, if true, most seriously weakens the argument above?

A. Tankers can easily be redesigned so that their use entails less risk of an oil spill.
B. Oil spills caused by tankers have generally been more serious than those caused by offshore operations.
C. The impact of offshore operations on the environment can be controlled by careful management.
D. Offshore operations usually damage the ocean floor, but tankers rarely cause such damage.
E. Importing oil on tankers is currently less expensive than drilling for it offshore.

21. In the last decade there has been a significant decrease in coffee consumption. During this same time, there has been increasing publicity about the adverse long-term effects on health of the caffeine in coffee. Therefore, the decrease in coffee consumption must have been caused by consumers' awareness of the harmful effects of caffeine.

Which of the following, if true, most seriously calls into question the explanation above?

A. On average, people consume 30 percent less coffee today than they did 10 years ago.
B. Heavy coffee drinkers may have mild withdrawal symptoms, such as headaches, for a day or so after significantly decreasing their coffee consumption.
C. Sales of specialty types of coffee have held steady as sales of regular brands have declined.
D. The consumption of fruit juices and caffeine-free herbal teas has increased over the past decade.
E. Coffee prices increased steadily in the past decade because of unusually severe frosts in coffee-growing nations.

22. Crowding on Mooreville's subway frequently leads to delays, because it is difficult for passengers to exit from the trains. Subway ridership is projected to increase by 20 percent over the next 10 years. The Mooreville Transit Authority plans to increase the number of daily train trips by only 5 percent over the same period. Officials predict that this increase is sufficient to ensure that the incidence of delays due to crowding does not increase.

Which of the following, if true, provides the strongest grounds for the officials' prediction?

A. By changing maintenance schedules, the Transit Authority can achieve the 5 percent increase in train trips without purchasing any new subway cars.
B. The Transit Authority also plans a 5 percent increase in the number of bus trips on routes that connect to subways.

C. For most commuters who use the subway system, there is no practical alternative public transportation available.
D. Most of the projected increase in ridership is expected to occur in off-peak hours when trains are now sparsely used.
E. The 5 percent increase in the number of train trips can be achieved without an equal increase in Transit Authority operational costs.

23. Installing scrubbers in smokestacks and switching to cleaner-burning fuel are the two methods available to Northern Power for reducing harmful emissions from its plants. Scrubbers will reduce harmful emissions more than cleaner-burning fuels will. Therefore, by installing scrubbers, Northern Power will be doing the most that can be done to reduce harmful emissions from its plants.

Which of the following is an assumption on which the argument depends?

A. Switching to cleaner-burning fuel will not be more expensive than installing scrubbers.
B. Northern Power can choose from among various kinds of scrubbers, some of which are more effective than others.
C. Northern Power is not necessarily committed to reducing harmful emissions from its plants.
D. Harmful emissions from Northern Power's plants cannot be reduced more by using both methods together than by the installation of scrubbers alone.
E. Aside from harmful emissions from the smokestacks of its plants, the activities of Northern Power do not cause significant air pollution.

24. Some anthropologists study modern-day societies of foragers in an effort to learn about our ancient ancestors who were also foragers. A flaw in this strategy is that forager societies are extremely varied. Indeed, any forager society with which anthropologists are familiar has had considerable contact with modern, non-forager societies.

Which of the following, if true, would most weaken the criticism made above of the anthropologists' strategy?

A. All forager societies throughout history have had a number of important features in common that are absent from other types of societies.
B. Most ancient forager societies either dissolved or made a transition to another way of life.
C. All anthropologists study one kind or another of modern-day society.
D. Many anthropologists who study modern-day forager societies do not draw inferences about ancient societies on the basis of their studies.
E. Even those modern-day forager societies that have not had significant contact with modern societies are importantly different from ancient forager societies.

25. If the county continues to collect residential trash at current levels, landfills will soon be overflowing and parkland will need to be used in order to create more space. Charging each household a fee for each pound of trash it puts out for collection will induce residents to reduce the amount of trash they create; this charge will, therefore, protect the remaining county parkland.

Which of the following is an assumption made in drawing the conclusion above?

  A. Residents will reduce the amount of trash they put out for collection by reducing the number of products they buy.
  B. The collection fee will not significantly affect the purchasing power of most residents, even if their households do not reduce the amount of trash they put out.
  C. The collection fee will not induce residents to dump their trash in the parklands illegally.
  D. The beauty of county parkland is an important issue for most of the county's residents.
  E. Landfills outside the county's borders could be used as dumping sites for the county's trash.

26. Although computers can enhance people's ability to communicate, computer games are a cause of underdeveloped communication skills in children. After-school hours spent playing computer games are hours not spent talking with people. Therefore, children who spend all their spare time playing these games have less experience in interpersonal communication than other children have.

The argument depends on which of the following assumptions?

  A. Passive activities such as watching television and listening to music do not hinder the development of communication skills in children.
  B. Most children have other opportunities, in addition to after-school hours, in which they can choose whether to play computer games or to interact with other people.
  C. Children who do not spend all of their afterschool hours playing computer games spend at least some of that time talking with other people.
  D. Formal instruction contributes little or nothing to children's acquisition of communication skills.
  E. The mental skills developed through playing computer games do not contribute significantly to children's intellectual development.

27. One variety of partially biodegradable plastic beverage container is manufactured from small bits of plastic bound together by a degradable bonding agent such as cornstarch. Since only the bonding agent degrades, leaving the small bits of plastic, no less plastic refuse per container is produced when such containers are discarded than when comparable nonbiodegradable containers are discarded.

Which of the following, if true, most strengthens the argument above?

A. Both partially biodegradable and non-biodegradable plastic beverage containers can be crushed completely flat by refuse compactors.
B. The partially biodegradable plastic beverage containers are made with more plastic than comparable nonbiodegradable ones in order to compensate for the weakening effect of the bonding agents.
C. Many consumers are ecology-minded and prefer to buy a product sold in the partially biodegradable plastic beverage containers rather in in nonbiodegradable containers even if the price is higher.
D. The manufacturing process for the partially biodegradable plastic beverage containers results in less plastic waste than the manufacturing process for nonbiodegradable plastic beverage containers.
E. Technological problems with recycling currently prevent the reuse as food or beverage containers of the plastic from either type of plastic beverage container.

28. Which of the following most logically completes the argument given below?

People in isolated rain-forest communities tend to live on a largely vegetarian diet, and they eat little salt. Few of them suffer from high blood pressure, and their blood pressure does not tend to increase with age, as is common in industrialized countries. Such people often do develop high blood pressure when they move to cities and adopt high-salt diets. Though suggestive these facts do not establish salt as the culprit in high blood pressure, however, because _____

A. Genetic factors could account for the lack of increase of blood pressure with age among such people.
B. People eating high-salt diets and living from birth in cities in industrialized societies generally have a tendency to have high blood pressure.
C. It is possible to have a low-salt diet while living in a city in an industrialized country.
D. There are changes in other aspects of diet when such people move to the city.
E. Salt is a necessity for human life, and death can occur when the body loses too much salt.

29. Even though most universities retain the royalties from faculty members' inventions, the faculty members retain the royalties from books and articles they write. Therefore, faculty members should retain the royalties from the educational computer software they develop.

The conclusion above would be more reasonably drawn if which of the following were inserted into the argument as an additional premise?

A. Royalties from inventions are higher than royalties from educational software programs.

B. Faculty members are more likely to produce educational software programs than inventions.
C. Inventions bring more prestige to universities than do books and articles.
D. In the experience of most universities, educational software programs are more marketable than are books and articles.
E. In terms of the criteria used to award royalties, educational software programs are more nearly comparable to books and articles than to inventions.

30. In order to withstand tidal currents, juvenile horseshoe crabs frequently burrow in the sand. Such burrowing discourages barnacles from clinging to their shells. When fully grown, however, the crabs can readily withstand tidal currents without burrowing, and thus they acquire substantial populations of barnacles. Surprisingly, in areas where tidal currents are very weak, juvenile horseshoe crabs are found not to have significant barnacle populations, even though they seldom burrow.

Which of the following, if true, most helps to explain the surprising finding?

A. Tidal currents do not themselves dislodge barnacles from the shells of horseshoe crabs.
B. Barnacles most readily attach themselves to horseshoe crabs in areas where tidal currents are weakest.
C. The strength of the tidal currents in a given location varies widely over the course of a day.
D. A very large barnacle population can significantly decrease the ability of a horseshoe crab to find food.
E. Until they are fully grown, horseshoe crabs shed their shells and grow new ones several times a year.

31. Red blood cells in which the malarial-fever parasite resides are eliminated from a person's body after 120 days. Because the parasite cannot travel to a new generation of red blood cells, any fever that develops in a person more than 120 days after that person has moved to a malaria-free region is not due to the malarial parasite.

Which of the following, if true, most seriously weakens the conclusion above?

A. The fever caused by the malarial parasite may resemble the fever caused by flu viruses.
B. The anopheles mosquito, which is the principal insect carrier of the malarial parasite, has been eradicated in many parts of the world.
C. Many malarial symptoms other than the fever, which can be suppressed with antimalarial medication, can reappear within 120 days after the medication is discontinued.

D. In some cases, the parasite that causes malarial fever travels to cells of the spleen, which are less frequently eliminated from a person's body than are red blood cells.
E. In any region infested with malaria-carrying mosquitoes there are individuals who appear to be immune to malaria.

32. When there is less rainfall than normal, the water level of Australian rivers falls and the rivers flow more slowly. Because algae whose habitat is river water grow best in slow-moving water, the amount of algae per unit of water generally increases when there has been little rain. By contrast, however, following a period of extreme drought, algae levels are low even in very slow-moving river water.

Which of the following, if true, does most to explain the contrast described above?

A. During periods of extreme drought, the populations of some of the species that feed on algae tend to fall.
B. The more slowly water moves, the more conducive its temperature is to the growth of algae.
C. When algae populations reach very high levels, conditions within the river can become toxic for some of the other species that normally live there.
D. Australian rivers dry up completely for short intervals in periods of extreme drought.
E. Except during periods of extreme drought, algae levels tend to be higher in rivers in which the flow has been controlled by damming than in rivers that flow freely.

33. Excavation of the ancient city of Kourion on the island of Cyprus revealed a pattern of debris and collapsed buildings typical of towns devastated by earthquakes. Archaeologists have hypothesized that the destruction was due to a major earthquake known to have occurred near the island in A.D. 365.

Which of the following, if true, most strongly supports the archaeologists' hypothesis?

A. Bronze ceremonial drinking vessels that are often found in graves dating from years proceeding and following A.D. 365 wee also found in several graves near Kourion.
B. No coins minted after A.D. 365 were found in Kourion, but coins minted before that year were found in abundance.
C. Most modern histories of Cyprus mention that an earthquake occurred near the island in A.D. 365.
D. Several small statues carved in styles current in Cyprus in the century between A.D. 300 and A.D. 400 were found in Kourion.
E. Stone inscriptions in a form of the Greek alphabet that was definitely used in Cyprus after A.D. 365 were found in Kourion.

34. Several industries have recently switched at least partly from older technologies powered by fossil fuels to new technologies powered by electricity. It is thus evident that less fossil fuel is being used as a result of the operations of these industries than would have been used if these industries had retained their older technologies.

Which of the following, if true, most strengthens the argument above?

A. Many of the industries that have switched at least partly to the new technologies have increased their output.
B. Less fossil fuel was used to manufacture the machinery employed in the new technologies than was originally used to manufacture the machinery employed in the older technologies.
C. More electricity is used by those industries that have switched at least partly to the new technologies than by those industries that have not switched.
D. Some of the industries that have switched at least partly to the new technologies still use primarily technologies that are powered by fossil fuels.
E. The amount of fossil fuel used to generate the electricity needed to power the new technologies in less than the amount that would have been used to power the older technologies.

35. Roland: The alarming fact is that 90 percent of the people in this country now report that they know someone who is unemployed.

Sharon: But a normal, moderate level of unemployment is 5 percent, with one out of 20 workers unemployed. So at any given time if a person knows approximately 50 workers, one or more will very likely be unemployed.

Sharon's argument relies on the assumption that

A. Normal levels of unemployment are rarely exceeded.
B. Unemployment is not normally concentrated in geographically isolated segments of the population.
C. The number of people who each know someone who is unemployed is always higher than 90 percent of the population.
D. Roland is not consciously distorting the statistics he presents.
E. Knowledge that a personal acquaintance is unemployed generates more fear of losing one' job than does knowledge of unemployment statistics.

36. In comparison to the standard typewriter keyboard, the EFCO keyboard, which places the most-used keys nearest the typist's strongest fingers, allows faster typing and results in less fatigue. Therefore, replacement of standard keyboards with the EFCO keyboard will result in an immediate reduction of typing costs.

Which of the following, if true, would most weaken the conclusion drawn above?

A. People who use both standard and EFCO keyboards report greater difficulty in the transition from the EFCO keyboard to the standard keyboard than in the transition from the standard keyboard than in the transition from the standard keyboard to the EFCO keyboard.
B. EFCO keyboards are no more expensive to manufacture than are standard keyboard and require less frequent repair than do standard keyboards.
C. The number of businesses and government agencies that use EFCO keyboards is increasing each year.
D. The more training and experience an employee has had with the standard keyboard, the more costly it is to train that employee to use the EFCO keyboard.
E. Novice typists can learn to use the EFCO keyboard in about the same amount of time that it takes them to learn to use the standard keyboard.

37. An overly centralised economy, not the changes in the climate, is responsible for the poor agricultural production in Country X since its new government came to power. Neighbouring Country Y has experienced the same climatic conditions, but while agricultural production has been falling in Country X, it has been rising in Country Y.

Which of the following, if true, would most weaken the argument above?

A. Industrial production also is declining in Country X.
B. Whereas Country Y is landlocked, Country X has a major seaport.
C. Both Country X and Country Y have been experiencing drought conditions.
D. The crops that have always been grown in Country X are different from those that have always been grown in Country Y.
E. Country X's new government instituted a centralized economy with the intention of ensuring an equitable distribution of goods.

38. Because no employee wants to be associated with bad news in the eyes of a superior, information about serious problems at lower levels is progressively softened and distorted as it goes up each step in the management hierarchy. The chief executive is, therefore, less well informed about problems at lower levels than are his or her subordinates at those levels.

The conclusion drawn above is based on the assumption that

A. Problems should be solved at the level in the management hierarchy at which they occur.
B. Employees should be rewarded for accurately reporting problems to their superiors.
C. Problem-solving ability is more important at higher levels than it is at lower levels of the management hierarchy.
D. Chief executives obtain information about problems at lower levels from no source other than their subordinates.

E. Some employees are more concerned about truth than about the way they are perceived by their superiors.

39. A recent report determined that although only 3 percent of drivers on Maryland highways equipped their vehicles with radar detectors, 33 percent of all vehicles ticketed for exceeding the speed limit were equipped with them. Clearly, drivers who equip their vehicles with radar detectors are more likely to exceed the speed limit regularly than are drivers who do not.

The conclusion drawn above depends on which of the following assumptions?

A. Drivers who equip their vehicles with radar detectors are less likely to be ticketed for exceeding the speed limit than are drivers who do not.
B. Drivers who are ticketed for exceeding the speed limit are more likely to exceed the speed limit regularly than are drivers who are not ticketed.
C. The number of vehicles that were equipped with radar detectors.
D. Many of the vehicles that were ticketed for exceeding the speed limit were ticketed more than once in the time period covered by the report.
E. Drivers on Maryland highways exceeded the speed limit more often than did drivers on other state highways not covered in the report.

40. When demand for a factory's products is high, more money is spent at the factory for safety precautions and machinery maintenance than when demand is low. Thus, the average number of on-the-job accidents per employee each month should be lower during periods when demand is high than when demand is low and less money is available for safety precautions and machinery maintenance.

Which of the following, if true about a factory when demand for its products is high, casts the most serious doubt on the conclusion drawn above?

A. Its employees ask for higher wages than they do at other times.
B. Its management hires new workers but lacks the time to train them properly.
C. Its employees are less likely to lose their jobs than they are at other times.
D. Its management sponsors a monthly safety award for each division in the factory.
E. Its old machinery is replaced with modern automated models.

41. Journalist: In physics journals, the number of articles reporting the results of experiments involving particle accelerators was lower last year that it had been in previous years. Several of the particle accelerators at major research institutions were out of service the year before last for repairs, so it is likely that the low number of articles was due to the decline in availability of particle accelerators.

Which of the following, if true, most seriously undermines the journalist's argument?

A. Every article based on experiments with particle accelerators that was submitted for publication last year actually was published.
B. The average time scientists must wait for access to a particle accelerator has declined over the last several years.
C. The number of physics journals was the same last year as in previous years.
D. Particle accelerators can be used for more than one group of experiments in any given year.
E. Recent changes in the editorial policies of several physics journals have decreased the likelihood that articles concerning particle-accelerator research will be accepted for publication.

42. Many people suffer an allergic reaction to certain sulphites, including those that are commonly added to wine as preservatives. However, since there are several winemakers who add sulphites to none of the wines they produce people who would like to drink wine but are allergic to sulphites can drink wines produced by these winemakers without risking an allergic reaction to sulphites.

Which of the following is an assumption on which the argument depends?

A. These winemakers have been able to duplicate the preservative effect produced by adding sulphites by means that do not involve adding any potentially allergenic substances to their wine.
B. Not all forms of sulphite are equally likely to produce the allergic reaction.
C. Wine is the only beverage to which sulphites are commonly added.
D. Apart from sulphites, there are no substances commonly present in wine that give rise to an allergic reaction.
E. Sulphites are not naturally present in the wines produced by these winemakers in amounts large enough to produce an allergic reaction in someone who drinks these wines.

43. Networks of blood vessels in bats' wings serve only to disperse heat generated in flight. This heat is generated only because bats flap their wings. Thus paleontologists' recent discovery that the winged dinosaur Sandactylus had similar networks of blood vessels in the skin of its wings provides evidence for the hypothesis that Sandactylus flew by flapping its wings, not just by gliding.

In the passage, the author develops the argument by

A. Forming the hypothesis that best explains several apparently conflicting pieces of evidence.
B. Reinterpreting evidence that had been used to support an earlier theory.
C. Using an analogy with a known phenomenon to draw a conclusion about an unknown phenomenon.
D. Speculating about how structures observed in present-day creatures might have developed from similar structures in creatures now extinct.

E. Pointing out differences in the physiological demands that flight makes on large, as opposed to small, creatures.

44. In the United States, of the people who moved from one state to another when they retired, the percentage who retired to Florida has decreased by three percentage points over the past ten years. Since many local businesses in Florida cater to retirees, these declines are likely to have a noticeably negative economic effect on these businesses and therefore on the economy of Florida.

Which of the flowing, if true, most seriously weakens the argument given?

A. People who moved from one state to another when they retired moved a greater distance, on average, last year than such people did ten years ago.
B. People were more likely to retire to North Carolina from another state last year than people were ten years ago.
C. The number of people who moved from one state to another when they retired has increased significantly over the past ten years.
D. The number of people who left Florida when they retired to live in another state was greater last year than it was ten years ago.
E. Florida attracts more people who move from one state to another when they retire than does any other state.

45. Environmentalist: The commissioner of the Fish and Game Authority would have the public believe that increases in the number of marine fish caught demonstrate that this resource is no longer endangered. This is a specious argument, as unsound as it would be to assert that the ever-increasing rate at which rain forests are being cut down demonstrates a lack of danger to that resource. The real cause of the increased fish-catch is a greater efficiency in using technologies that deplete resources.

The environmentalist's statements, if true, best support which of the following as a conclusion?

A. The use of technology is the reason for the increasing encroachment of people on nature.
B. It is possible to determine how many fish are in the sea in some way other than by catching fish.
C. The proportion of marine fish that are caught is as high as the proportion of rain forest trees that are cut down each year.
D. Modern technologies waste resources by catching inedible fish.
E. Marine fish continue to be an endangered resource.

46. In the country of Veltria, the past two years' broad economic recession has included a business downturn in the clothing trade, where sales are down by about 7 percent as compared to two years ago. Clothing wholesalers have found, however, that the proportion of credit extended to retailers that was paid off on time fell sharply in the first year of the recession but returned to its prerecession level in the second year.

Which of the following, if true, most helps to explain the change between the first and the second year of the recession in the proportion of credit not paid off on time?

    A. The total amount of credit extended to retailers by clothing wholesalers increased between the first year of the recession and the second year.
    B. Between the first and second years of the recession, clothing retailers in Veltria saw many of their costs, rent and utilities in particular increase.
    C. Of the considerable number of clothing retailers in Veltria who were having financial difficulties before the start of the recession, virtually all were forced to go out of business during its first year.
    D. Clothing retailers in Veltria attempted to stimulate sales in the second year of the recession by discounting merchandise.
    E. Relatively recession-proof segments of the clothing trade, such as work clothes, did not suffer any decrease in sales during the first year of the recession.

47. Commentator: The theory of trade retaliation states that countries closed out of any of another country's markets should close some of their own markets to the other country in order to pressure the other country to reopen its markets. If every country acted according to this theory, no country would trade with any other.

The commentator's argument relies on which of the following assumptions?

    A. No country actually acts according to the theory of trade retaliation.
    B. No country should block any of its markets to foreign trade.
    C. Trade disputes should be settled by international tribunal.
    D. For any two countries, at least one has some market closed to the other.
    E. Countries close their markets to foreigners to protect domestic producers.

48. Studies in restaurants show that the tips left by customers who pay their bill in cash tend to be larger when the bill is presented on a tray that bears a credit card logo. Consumer psychologists hypothesize that simply seeing a credit-card logo makes many credit-card holders willing to spend more because it reminds them that their spending power exceeds the cash they have immediately available.

Which of the following, if true, most strongly supports the psychologists' interpretation of the studies?

    A. The effect noted in the studies is not limited to patrons who have credit cards.
    B. Patrons who are under financial pressure from their credit-card obligations tend to tip less when presented with a restaurant bill on a tray with a credit-card logo than when the tray has no logo.
    C. In virtually all of the cases in the studies, the patrons who paid bills in cash did not possess credit cards.

D. In general, restaurant patrons who pay their bills in cash leave larger tips than do those who pay by credit card.
E. The percentage of restaurant bills paid with a given brand of credit card increases when that credit card's logo is displayed on the tray with which the bill is presented.

49. Which of the following most logically completes the argument?

The irradiation of food kills bacteria and thus retards spoilage. However, it also lowers the nutritional value of many foods. For example, irradiation destroys a significant percentage of whatever vitamin B1 a food may contain. Proponents of irradiation point out that irradiation is no worse in this respect than cooking. However, this fact is either beside the point, since much irradiated food is eaten raw, or else misleading since_____

A. Many of the proponents of irradiation are food distributors who gain from foods' having a longer shelf life.
B. It is clear that killing bacteria that may be present on food is not the only effect that irradiation has.
C. Cooking is usually the final step in preparing food for consumption, whereas irradiation serves to ensure a longer shelf life for perishable foods.
D. Certain kinds of cooking are, in fact, even more destructive of vitamin B1 than carefully controlled irradiation is.
E. For food that is both irradiated and cooked, the reduction of vitamin B1 associated with either process individually is compounded.

50. For a trade embargo against a particular country to succeed, a high degree of both international accord and ability to prevent goods from entering or leaving that country must be sustained. A total blockade of Patria's ports is necessary to an embargo, but such an action would be likely to cause international discord over the embargo.

The claims above, if true, most strongly support which of the following conclusions?

A. The balance of opinion is likely to favour Patria in the event of a blockade.
B. As long as international opinion is unanimously against Patria, a trade embargo is likely to succeed.
C. A naval blockade of Patria's ports would ensure that no goods enter or leave Patria.
D. Any trade embargo against Patria would be likely to fail at some time.
E. For a blockade of Patria's ports to be successful, international opinion must be unanimous.

51. The cost of producing radios in Country Q is 10 percent less than the cost of producing radios in Country Y. Even after transportation fees and tariff charges are added, it is still cheaper for a company to import radios from Country Q to country Y than to produce radios in Country Y.

The statements above, if true, best support which of the following assertions?

A. Labour costs in Country Q are 10 percent below those in Country Y.
B. Importing radios from Country Q to Country Y will eliminate 10 percent of the manufacturing jobs in Country Y.
C. The tariff on a radio imported from Country Q to Country Y is less than 10 percent of the cost of manufacturing the radio in Country Y.
D. The fee for transporting a radio from Country Q to Country Y is more than 10 percent of the cost of manufacturing the radio in Country Q.
E. It takes 10 percent less time to manufacture a radio in Country Q than it does in Country Y.

52. Although the discount stores in Goreville's central shopping district are expected to close within five years as a result of competition from a SpendLess discount department store that just opened, those locations will not stay vacant for long. In the five years since the opening of Colson's a non-discount department store, a new store has opened at the location of every store in the shopping district that closed because it could not compete with Colson's.

Which of the following, if true, most seriously weakens the argument?

A. Many customers of Colson's are expected to do less shopping there than they did before the SpendLess store opened.
B. Increasingly, the stores that have opened in the central shopping district since Colson's opened have been discount stores.
C. At present, the central shopping district has as many stores operating in it as it ever had.
D. Over the course of the next five years, it is expected that Goreville's population will grow at a faster rate than it has for the past several decades.
E. Many stores in the central shopping district sell types of merchandise that are not available at either SpendLess or Colson's.

53. The average normal infant born in the United States weights between 12 and 14 pounds at the age of three months. Therefore, if a three-month-old child weighs only 10 pounds, its weight gain has been below the United States average.

Which of the following indicates a flaw in the reasoning above?

A. Weight is only one measure of normal infant development.
B. Some three-month-old-children weigh as much as 17 pounds.
C. It is possible for a normal child to weigh 10 pounds at birth.
D. The phrase "below average" does not necessarily mean insufficient.
E. Average weight gain is not the same as average weight.

54. Springfield Fire Commissioner: The vast majority of false fire alarms are prank calls made anonymously from fire alarm boxes on street corners. Since virtually everyone

has access to a private telephone, these alarm boxes have outlived their usefulness. Therefore, we propose to remove the boxes. Removing the boxes will reduce the number of prank calls without hampering people's ability to report a fire.

Which of the following, if true, most strongly supports the claim that the proposal, if carried out, will have the announced effect?

- A. The fire department traces all alarm calls made from private telephones and records where they came from.
- B. Maintaining the fire alarm boxes costs Springfield approximately $5 million annually.
- C. A telephone call can provide the fire department with more information about the nature and size of a fire than can an alarm placed from an alarm box.
- D. Responding to false alarms significantly reduces the fire department's capacity for responding to fires.
- E. On any given day, a significant percentage of the public telephones in Springfield are out of service.

55. The difficulty with the proposed high-speed train line is that a used plane can be bought for one-third the price of the train line, and the plane, which is just as fast, can fly anywhere. The train would be a fixed linear system, and we live in a world that is spreading out in all directions and in which consumers choose the free-wheel systems (cars, buses, aircraft), which do not have fixed routes. Thus a sufficient market for the train will not exist.

Which of the following, if true, most severely weakens the argument presented above?

- A. Cars, buses and planes require the efforts of drivers and pilots to guide them, whereas the train will be guided mechanically.
- B. Cars and buses are not nearly as fast as the high-speed train will be.
- C. Planes are not a free-wheel system because they can fly only between airports, which are less convenient for consumers than the high-speed train's stations would be.
- D. The high-speed train line cannot use currently underutilized train stations in large cities.
- E. For long trips, most people prefer to fly rather than to take ground-level transportation.

56. The average hourly wage of television assemblers in Vernland has long been significantly lower than that in neighbouring Borodia. Since Borodia dropped all tariffs on Vernlandian televisions three years ago, the number of televisions sold annually in Borodia has not changed. However, recent statistics show a drop in the number of television assemblers in Borodia. Therefore, updated trade statistics will probably

indicate that the number of televisions Borodia imports annually from Vernland has increased.

Which of the following is an assumption on which the argument depends?

- A. The number of television assemblers in Vernland has increased by at least as such as the number of television assemblers in Borodia has decreased.
- B. Televisions assembled in Vernland have features that televisions assembled in Borodia do not have.
- C. The average number of hours it takes a Borodian television assembler to assemble a television has not decreased significantly during the past three years.
- D. The number of televisions assembled annually in Vernland has increased significantly during the past three years.
- E. The difference between the hourly wage of television assemblers in Vernland and the hourly wage of television assemblers in Borodia is likely to decrease in the next few years.

57. Guidebook writer: I have visited hotels through the country and have noticed that in those built before 1930 the quality of the original carpentry work is generally superior to that in hotels built afterward. Clearly carpenters working on hotels before 1930 typically worked with more skill, care, and effort than carpenters who have worked on hotels built subsequently.

Which of the following, if true, most seriously weakens the guidebook writer's argument?

- A. The quality of original carpentry in hotels is generally far superior to the quality of original carpentry in other structures, such as houses and stores.
- B. Hotels built since 1930 can generally accommodate more guests than those built before 1930.
- C. The materials available to carpenters working before 1930 were not significantly different in quality from the materials available to carpenters working after 1930.
- D. The better the quality of original carpentry in a building, the less likely that building is to fall into disuse and be demolished.
- E. The average length of apprenticeship for carpenters has declined significantly since 1930.

58. Northern Air has dozens of flights daily into and out of Belleville Airport, which is highly congested. Northern Air depends for its success on economy and quick turnaround and consequently is planning to replace its large planes with Skybuses, whose novel aerodynamic design is extremely fuel efficient. The Skybus's fuel efficiency results in both lower fuel costs and reduced time spent refuelling.

Which of the following, if true, could present the most serious disadvantage for Northern Air in replacing their large planes with Skybuses?

> A. The Skybus would enable Northern Air to schedule direct flights to destinations that currently require stops for refuelling.
> B. Aviation fuel is projected to decline in price over the next several years.
> C. The fuel efficiency of the Skybus would enable Northern Air to eliminate refuelling at some of its destinations, but several mechanics would lose their jobs.
> D. None of Northern Air's competitors that use Belleville Airport are considering buying Skybuses.
> E. The aerodynamic design of the Skybus causes turbulence behind it when taking off that forces other planes on the runway to delay their take-offs.

59. It is true of both men and women that those who marry as young adults live longer than those who never marry. This does not show that marriage causes people to live longer, since, as compared with other people of the same age, young adults who are about to get married have fewer of the unhealthy habits that can cause a person to have a shorter life, most notably smoking and immoderate drinking of alcohol.

Which of the following, if true, most strengthens the argument above?

> A. Marriage tends to cause people to engage less regularly in sports that involve risk of bodily harm.
> B. A married person who has an unhealthy habit is more likely to give up that habit than a person with the same habit who is unmarried.
> C. A person who smokes is much more likely than a non-smoker to marry a person who smokes at the time of marriage, and the same is true for people who drink alcohol immoderately.
> D. Among people who marry as young adults, most of those who give up an unhealthy habit after marriage do not resume the habit later in life.
> E. Among people who as young adults neither drink alcohol immoderately nor smoke, those who never marry live as long as those who marry.

60. The earliest Mayan pottery found at Colha, in Belize, is about 3,000 years old. Recently, however, 4,500 year old stone agricultural implements were unearthed at Colha. These implements resemble Mayan stone implements of a much later period also found at Colha. Moreover, the implements' designs are strikingly different from the designs of stone implements produced by other cultures known to have inhabited the area in prehistoric times. Therefore, there were surely Mayan settlements in Colha 4,500 years ago.

Which of the following, if true, most seriously weakens the argument?

> A. Ceramic ware is not known to have been used by the Mayan people to make agricultural implements.

B. Carbon-dating of corn pollen in Colha indicates that agriculture began there around 4,500 years ago.
C. Archaeological evidence indicates that some of the oldest stone implements found at Colha were used to cut away vegetation after controlled burning of trees to open areas of swampland for cultivation.
D. Successor cultures at a given site often adopt the style of agricultural implements used by earlier inhabitants of the same site.
E. Many religious and social institutions of the Mayan people who inhabited Colha 3,000 years ago relied on a highly developed system of agricultural symbols.

61. Codex Berinensis, a Florentine copy of an ancient Roman medical treatise, is undated but contains clues to when it was produced. Its first 80 pages are by a single copyist, but the remaining 20 pages are by three different copyists, which indicate some significant disruption. Since a letter in handwriting identified as that of the fourth copyist mentions a plague that killed many people in Florence in 1148. Codex Berinensis was probably produced in that year.

Which of the following, if true, most strongly supports the hypothesis that Codex Berinensis was produced in 1148?

A. Other than Codex Berinensis, there are no known samples of the handwriting of the first three copyists.
B. According to the account by the fourth copyist, the plague went on for 10 months.
C. A scribe would be able to copy a page of text the size and style of Codex Berinensis in a day.
D. There was only one outbreak of plague in Florence in the 1100s.
E. The number of pages of Codex Berinensis produced by a single scribe becomes smaller with each successive change of copyist.

62. The spacing of the four holes on a fragment of a bone flute excavated at a Neanderthal campsite is just what is required to play the third through sixth notes of the diatonic scale – the seven-note musical scale used in much of Western music since the Renaissance.

Musicologists, therefore, hypothesize that the diatonic music scale was developed and used thousands of years before it was adopted by Western musicians.

Which of the following, if true, most strongly supports the hypothesis?

A. Bone flutes were probably the only musical instrument made by Neanderthals.
B. No musical instrument that is known to have used a diatonic scale is of an earlier date than the flute found at the Neanderthal campsite.

C. The flute was made from a cave-bear bone and the campsite at which the flute fragment was excavated was in a cave that also contained skeletal remains of cave bears.
D. Flutes are the simplest wind instrument that can be constructed to allow playing a diatonic scale.
E. The cave-bear leg bone used to make the Neanderthal flute would have been long enough to make a flute capable of playing a complete diatonic scale.

63. Outsourcing is the practice of obtaining from an independent supplier a product or service that a company has previously provided for itself. Since a company's chief objective is to realize the highest possible year-end profits, any product or service that can be obtained from an independent supplier for less than it would cost the company to provide the product or service on its own should be outsourced.

Which of the following, if true, most seriously weakens the argument?

A. If a company decides to use independent suppliers for a product, it can generally exploit the vigorous competition arising among several firms that are interested in supplying that product.
B. Successful outsourcing requires a company to provide its suppliers with information about its products and plans that can fall into the hands of its competitors and give them a business advantage.
C. Certain tasks, such as processing a company's payroll are commonly outsourced, whereas others, such as handling the company's core business, are not.
D. For a company to provide a product or service for itself as efficiently as an independent supplier can provide it, the managers involved need to be as expert in the area of that product or service as the people in charge of that product or service at an independent supplier are.

When a company decides to use an independent supplier for a product or service, the independent supplier sometimes hires members of the company's staff who formerly made the product or provided the service that the independent supplier now supplies.

64. In recent years, many cabinetmakers have been winning acclaim as artists. But since furniture must be useful, cabinetmakers must exercise their craft with an eye to the practical utility of their product. For this reason, cabinetmaking is not art.

Which of the following is an assumption that supports drawing the conclusion above from the reason given for that conclusion?

A. Some furniture is made to be placed in museums, where it will not be used by anyone.
B. Some cabinetmakers are more concerned than others with the practical utility of the products they produce.

C. Cabinetmakers should be more concerned with the practical utility of their products than they currently are.
D. An object is not art if its maker pays attention to the object's practical utility
E. Artists are not concerned with the monetary value of their products.

65. The Fanto Corporation, a leading computer chip manufacturer, is currently developing a new chip, which is faster and more efficient than any computer chip currently in use. The new chip will be released for sale in twelve months. Fantos' market research has shown that initial sales of the new chip would be maximised by starting to advertise now, but the company has decided to wait another six months before doing so.

Which of the following, if true, provides the Fanto Corporation with the best reason for postponing advertising its new chip?

A. Some computer users are reluctant to purchase new computer products when they are first released.
B. The cost of an advertising campaign capable of maximising initial sales of the new chip would be no greater than campaigns previously undertaken by Fanto.
C. Advertising the new chip now will significantly decrease sales of Fantos' current line of computer chips.
D. Fantos' major rivals in the computer chip business are developing a chip with similar capabilities to the new Fanto chip.
E. Taking full advantage of the new chip will require substantial adjustments in other segments of the computer industry.

Answers to Practice Questions – Numerical

1.

The budget for four months is

$\frac{12600}{12}$ x 4 = $4,200. Thus the project was $4,580 - $4,200 = $380 over budget for the first four months

The correct answer is A.

2.

Convert the words into symbols and solve the equation:

5+8+12+15 = 3+4+ x + (x+3)

40 = 2 x + 10

30 = 2 x

15 = x

The correct answer is B

3.

Substitute the value for n given in each answer choice into the expression, and then simplify to determine whether or not that value results in an interger.

A $\frac{100+1}{1}$ = 101 Integer

B $\frac{100+2}{2}$ = 51 Integer

C $\frac{100+3}{3}$ = 34.33 NOT an Integer

D $\frac{100+4}{4}$ = 26 Integer

E $\frac{100+5}{5}$ = 21 Integer

Another method is to rewrite the given expression, $\frac{100+n}{n}$ as $\frac{100}{n} + \frac{n}{n} = \frac{100}{n} + 1$

This shows that the given expression is an integer exactly when $\frac{100}{n}$ is an integer. Since 100 is not divisible by 3, but 100 is divisible by 1, 2, 4, and 5, it follows that n=3

The correct answer is C

4.

Since Floor X is a rectangle, its area is (width)(length) = (12)(18). It is given that this also the area of Floor Y. So if L is the length of Floor Y it follows that 9L = (12)(18) thus L = 24.

The correct answer is E.

5.

From the table, there are 5 employees each with a salary of $20,000, 4 employees each with a salary of $22,000, and so on. The average (arithmetic mean) for all 20 employees is then

$$= \frac{5(20000)+4(22000)+8(25000)+3(30000)}{20}$$

= 23,900

The correct answer is C

6.

Each case has *bc* boxes, each of which has 100 paper clips. The total number of paper clips in 2 cases is thus 2(*bc*)(100) = 200*bc*.

The correct answer is C

7.

This is a question which could take some candidates a lot of time as they tried to work accurately and precisely. But the question gives you a big hint – it asks "approximately". Given the question is looking for an approximation there is no need to be precise.

The very first thing we know is that the water has increased by 14bn gallons, so we can immediately ignore answers A and B because these answers are implausible given the information at hand.

We know 138 = 82%, so let's approximate that:

$1\% = \frac{140}{80} = \frac{7}{4}$

All I have done here is round the 138 and the 82 to more manageable numbers.

Now in order to determine how short the tank was before the rainfall I calculate the following:

$14 + (18 \times 1\frac{3}{4}) = 14 + (18 \times 1) + (18 \times \frac{3}{4})$

But now look back at the answer choices! I know this answer is going to be greater than 32 and only one of the remaining three answers is greater than 32 so I can select choice E here and move on having saved some valuable time.

The correct answer is E

8.

Since $\frac{1}{10}$ percent is $\frac{1}{1000}$, the difference asked for is $(\frac{1}{10})(5000) - (\frac{1}{1000})(5000) = 500 - 5 = 495$

The correct answer is D

9.

Letting x represent the total value of the item, convert the words to symbols and solve the equation.

7% of value in excess of $1,000 = 87.50

$0.07(x - 1,000) = 87.50$

$x - 1,000 = 1,250$

$x = 2,250$

The correct answer is C

10.

Since average = $\frac{Sum\ of\ values}{Number\ of\ Values}$ the information about the two shipments of packages can be expressed as:

Average = $\frac{8(12\frac{3}{8}) + 4(15\frac{1}{4})}{12} = \frac{8(\frac{99}{8}) + 4(\frac{61}{4})}{12} = \frac{99 + 61}{12} = 13\frac{1}{3}$

Let's imagine this question showed up late in the exam and you were struggling for time. You know the average weight has to be between the weight of the two averages given, but three of the answer choices greater than the higher weight! This means you are left with only two answers and you could choose now to take a guess and move on.

The correct answer is A

11.

Calculate the squared and the cubed term, and then add the three terms.

$0.1 + (0.1)^2 + (0.1)^3 = 0.1 + 0.01 + 0.001 = 0.111$

The correct answer is B

12.

When all the dimensions of a three-dimensional object are changed by a factor of 2, the capacity, or volume, changes by a factor of $(2)(2)(2) = 2^3 = 8$. Thus the capacity of the second sandbox is $10(8) = 80$ cubic feet.

The correct answer is D

13.

Since half of the 40 dozen rolls were sold by noon, then $\frac{1}{2}(40) = 20$ dozen rolls were left to be sold after noon. Because 80 percent of those 20 were sold, $100 - 80 = 20$ percent of them or $20(0.20) = 4$ dozen rolls had not been sold when the bakery closed.

The correct answer is D

14.

The ratio 2 to $\frac{1}{3}$ is the same as $\frac{2}{1} = 2\left(\frac{3}{1}\right) = 6$, which is the same as a ratio of 6 to 1.

The correct answer is A

15.

The simplest way to solve this problem is to choose a prime number greater than 3 and divide its square by 12 to see what the remainder is. For example, if $n = 5$, then $n^2 = 25$, and the remainder is 1 when 25 is divided by 12. A second prime number can be used to check the results. For example, if $n = 7$, then $n^2 = 49$, and the remainder is 1 when 49 is divided by 12. Because only one of the answer choices can be correct, the remainder must be 1.

For the more mathematically inclined, consider the remainder when each prime number n greater than 3 is divided by 6. The remainder cannot be 0 because that would imply that n is divisible by 6, which is impossible since n is a prime number. The remainder cannot be 3 because that would imply that n is divisible by 3, which is impossible since n is a prime number greater than 3. Therefore, the only possible remainders when a prime number n greater than 3 is divided by 6 are 1 and 5. Thus, n has the form $6q + 1$ or $6q + 5$, where q is an integer, and, therefore, n^2 has the form $36q^2 + 12q + 1 = 12(3q^2 + q) + 1$ or $36q^2 + 60q + 25 = 12(3q^2 + 5q + 2) + 1$. In either case, n^2 has a remainder of 1 when divided by 12.

The correct answer is B

16.

Perform the arithmetic calculations as follows:

$$\frac{1}{1+\frac{1}{3}} - \frac{1}{1+\frac{1}{2}}$$

$$= \frac{1}{\frac{4}{3}} - \frac{1}{\frac{3}{2}}$$

$$= \frac{3}{4} - \frac{2}{3}$$

$$= \frac{1}{12}$$

The correct answer is D

17.

Build an equation to express the given information and solve for the answer. Let x = length of the longer piece of rope in feet.

Thus $x + (x + 18) = 40$ is the entire length of the rope in feet.

$2x + 18 = 40$ combine like terms

$2x = 22$ subtract 18 from both sides

$x = 11$ divide both sides by 2

The correct answer is B

18.

The average of the student's first 4 test scores is 78, so the sum of the first 4 test scores is 4(78) = 312. If x represents the fifth test score, then the sum of all 5 test scores is 312 + x and the average of all 5 test scores is $\frac{312+x}{5}$ but the average of these 5 tests must equal 80 so

$$\frac{312+x}{5} = 80$$

312 + x = 400

x = 88

A quick route to this answer would be to see that the average of the first 4 is 2% short of 80%. Thus we need an extra 2% for each of these 4 tests plus a final extra 2% in test 5 to pull the overall average up to 80. Thus 5 x 2% = 10% which is the extra score we need over 78% to get an overall average of 80%.

The correct answer is E

19.

Let *m* represent the number of minutes it takes John to type *y* words. In this rate problem, the number of words typed = (typing rate)(time).

Thus, $y = xm$, or $m = \frac{y}{x}$

The correct answer is B

20.

Vertical angles are congruent, so 150 = 150 = 300 degrees of he circle are not shaded. Thus 60 degrees of it is, or

$$\frac{60}{360} = \frac{1}{6}$$

The correct answer is C

21.

Since $\frac{1}{9} < \frac{1}{8}, \frac{7}{8} + \frac{1}{9} < \frac{7}{8} + \frac{1}{8} = 1$, and answer choices C, D, and E can be eliminated.

Since

$\frac{7}{8} > \frac{6}{8} = \frac{3}{4}, \frac{7}{8} + \frac{1}{9} > \frac{3}{4}$, and answer choice A can be eliminated. Thus, $\frac{3}{4} < \frac{7}{8} + \frac{1}{9} < 1$.

The correct answer is B.

22.
Perform the arithmetic calculations as follows:

$1 - (\frac{1}{2} - \frac{2}{3}) = 1 - (\frac{3}{6} - \frac{4}{6})$

$= 1 - (-\frac{1}{6})$

$= 1 + \frac{1}{6}$

$= \frac{7}{6}$

The correct answer is B.

23.
The total number of seeds that germinated was 200 (0.57) + 300 (0.42) = 114 + 126 = 240. Because this was out 500 seeds planted, the percent of the total planted that germinated was $\frac{240}{500}$ = 0.48, or 48.0%.

The correct answer is C.

24.

Let x represent the people over 21. Then $3x$ represents the number of people 21 or under, and $x + 3x = 4x$ represents the total population. Thus the ratio of those 21 or under to the total population is $\frac{3x}{4x} = \frac{3}{4}$, or 3 to 4.

The correct answer is E.

25.

If Chris packed 60 percent of the boxes, then Kelly packed 100 − 60 = 40 percent of the boxes. The ratio of the number of boxes Kelly packed to the number Chris packed is $\frac{40\%}{60\%} = \frac{2}{3}$.

The correct answer is E.

26.

Using the formula $\frac{sum\ of\ n\ values}{n} = average$, the average of the first set of numbers is 30. Thus the average of 20, 40 and another number, x, must be equal to 25. Thus

$$\frac{20 + 40 + x}{3} = 25$$

Solving through we find x = 15

The correct answer is A.

27.

Let x be the number of grams of glucose in the 45 cubic centimeters of solution. The proportion comparing the glucose in the 45 cubic centimeters to the given information about the 15 grams of glucose in the entire 100 cubic centimeters of solution can be expressed as $\frac{x}{45} = \frac{15}{100}$ and so 100x = 675 or x = 6.75.

The correct answer is E.

28.

The first year's increase of 10 percent can be expressed as 1.10; the second year's increase of 5 percent can be expressed as 1.05; and the third year's decrease of 10 percent can be expressed as 0.90. Multiply the original value of the account by each of these yearly changes.

10,000(1.10)(1.05)(0.90) = 10,395

The correct answer is B

29.

If each apple sold for $0.70, each banana sold for $0.50, and the total purchase price was $6.30, then 0.70x + 0.50y = 6.30, where x and y are positive integers representing the number of apples and bananas, respectively, the customer purchased.

0.70 x 0.50y = 6.30

0.50y = 6.30 − 0.70x

0.50y = 0.70(9 − x)

$y = \frac{7}{5}(9 - x)$

Since y must be an integer, 9 − x must be divisible by 5. Furthermore, both x and y must be positive integers. For x = 1,2,3,4,5,6,7,8, the corresponding values of 9 − x are 8,7,6,5,4,3,2, and 1. Only one of these, 5, is divisible by 5.

Therefore, x = 4 and y = 7 (9 − 4) = 7 and the total number of apples and bananas the customer purchased is 4 + 7 = 11.

The correct answer is B.

30.

If F, S, T and R represent the number of first, second, third and fourth graders, respectively, then the given rations are:

(i) S/R = 8/5

(ii) F/S = 3/4

(iii) T/R = 3/2

The desired ratios is F/T.

From (ii) we find $F = \frac{3}{4}S$ and from (i) that $S = \frac{8}{5}R$

Combining these results leads to $F = \frac{6}{5}R$, at which point we rearrange (iii) to $T = \frac{3}{2}R$.

Now we have both F and T in terms of R and we want the ratio of F/T which is equal to

$$\frac{F}{T} = \frac{\frac{6}{5}R}{\frac{3}{2}R} = \frac{4}{5}$$

Thus, **the correct answer is E.**

31.

This question is simply examining your knowledge of lowest common multiples.

The correct answer is B.

32.

Since the ratio is 5:2:1, let 5× be the money allocated to household expenses, 2× be the money allocated to miscellaneous items. The given information can then be expressed in the following equation and solved for ×.

5× + 2× + 1× = $1,800

8× = $1,800   Combine like terms

× = $225   Divide both sides by 8

The money allocated to food is

2× = 2($225) = $450.

The correct answer is D.

33.

Let *m* be the number of men on the board and *w* be the number of women on the board. According to the problem,

w = m + 4   because there are 4 more women than men and

w + m = 10   because the board has a total of 10 members.

Substituting *m* + 4 for *w* in the second equation gives:

m + m + 4 = 10

2m + 4 = 10   combine like terms

2m = 6   subtract 4 from both sides

m = 3   divide both sides by 2

Using the first equation, w = m + 4 = 3 + 4 = 7 women on the board.

This problem can also be solved without algebra by listing the *(m,w)* possibilities for w = m+ 4. These possibilities are (0,4), (1,5), (2m6)m (3m7)m etc, and hence the pair in which m + w = 10 is (3,7).

The correct answer is D.

34.

Let f be the factor by which the amount of bacteria present increased every 3 hours. Then, from the table, $10.0f = x$ and $xf = 14.4$. Substituting $10.0f$ for x in the second equation gives

$(10.0f)f = 14.4$

$10.0f^2 = 14.4$

$f^2 = 1.44$

$f = 1.2$ [Note: This should be clear as $12^2 = 144$]

and then $x = 10.0(1.2) = 12.0$.

The correct answer is A.

35.

Let m represent the price of each map and b represent the price of each book. Then the given information can be represented by the system

(i) $12m + 10b = 38$ and,

(ii) $20m + 15b = 60$

Multiplying (i) by -3/2 gives $-18m - 15b = -57$ and then adding the two equations gives $2m = 3$ or $m = 1.5$.

Thus, each map sells for $1.50. Then,

$12(1.50) + 10b = 38$

$18 + 10b = 38$

$10b = 20$

$b = 2$

So, each book sells for $2.00 and each map sells for $1.50, which is $0.50 less than each book.

The correct answer is B.

36.

The percent increase in sales from last year to this year is 100 times the quotient of the difference in sales for the two years divided by the sales last year. Thus, the percent increase is

$$\frac{385-320}{320} \times 100 = \frac{65}{320} \times 100$$

$$= \frac{13}{64} \times 100 \approx \frac{13}{65} \times 100 = \frac{1}{5} \times 100 = 20\%$$

The correct answer is C.

37.

Letting v be the number of registered voters in the city, then the information that 60% of the registered voters are Democrats can be expressed as $0.60v$. From this, it can be stated that $1.00v - 0.60v = 0.40v$ are Republicans. The percentage of Democrats and the percentage of Republicans who are expected to vote for Candidate A can then be expressed as $(0.75)(0.60v) + (0.20)(0.40v)$. Simplify the expression to determine the total percentage of voters expected to vote for Candidate A.

$(0.75)(0.60v) + (0.20)(0.40v)$

$= 0.45v + 0.08v$

$= 0.53v$

The correct answer is B.

38.

The mass ratio of oxygen to water is $\frac{oxygen}{oxygen+hydrogen} = \frac{16}{16+2} = \frac{16}{18} = \frac{8}{9}$

Now simply solve $144 \times \frac{8}{9} = 128$.

The correct answer is D.

39.

Let s be the present number of students, and let t be the present number of teachers. According to the problem, the following two equations apply:

$\frac{30}{1} = \frac{s}{t}$ Current student to teacher ratio

$\frac{s+50}{t+5} = \frac{25}{1}$ Future student to teacher ratio

Solving the first equation for s gives s = 30t. Substitute this value of s into the second equation and solve for t.

$$\frac{30t+50}{t+5} = \frac{25}{1}$$

$30t + 50 = 25t + 125$

5t = 75

t = 15

The correct answer is E.

40.

For simplicity, suppose there are 100 members in the study group. Since 60 percent of the members are women, there are 60 women in the group. Also, 45 percent of the women are lawyers so there are 0.45(60) = 27 women lawyers in the study group. Therefore the probability of selecting a woman lawyer is $\frac{27}{100}$ = 0.27

The correct answer is C.

41.

The ratio of royalties to sales for the first $20m in sales is $\frac{3}{20}$. The ratio for the next $108m in sales is $\frac{9}{108} = \frac{1}{12}$. The percent decrease in the royalties sales ratio is calculated by determining what the percentage change when 3/20 falls to 1/12. This would take some time to calculate and the fractions are tricky to deal with, making a mistake more likely. Instead it may be easier to factor both number up by 60x (The lowest common multiple of 20 and 12) and work with these numbers instead. This means we now need to calculated the percentage decrease when 9 falls to 5 which is;

$\frac{9-5}{9} = \frac{4}{9} \approx 44\%$.

Choice C is the only close answer to this and is the correct answer. (Remember, this question uses the word approximately!)

42.

Two candy bars at the regular price cost $0.80. The sale price is $0.05 less. Thus the percentage reduction is $\frac{0.05}{0.80} \equiv \frac{5}{80} = \frac{1}{16} = 6.25\%$

Hint: Working out $\frac{1}{16}$ as a percentage is remarkably easy. If you know $\frac{1}{4}$ is 25%, half of this is $\frac{1}{8}$ or 12.5% and thus $\frac{1}{16}$ is simply 6.25%.

The correct answer is B.

43.

To determine the area of the trim, find the area of the unshaded portions of the door and subtract this from the door's total area. The width of each unshaded rectangle is the width of the door minus two trim strips, or 6 – 2 = 4 feet. The amount of height available for both unshaded rectangles is the height of the door minus three trim strips, or 8 – 3 =

5 feet. Thus, the area of the unshaded portions is 4 x 5 = 20 square feet. The area of the entire door is 6 x 8 = 48 square feet, so the area of the trim is 48 − 20 = 28 square feet. Therefore, the fraction of the do00r's front surface that is covered by the trim is $\frac{28}{48} = \frac{7}{12}$.

The correct answer is D.

44.

Let M be Mary's income, T be Tim's income, and J be Juan's income. Mary's income is 60 percent more than Tim's, so $M = T + 0.60T = 1.60T$. Since Tim's income is 40 percent less than Juan's income, Tim's income equals 100-40= 60 percent of Juan's income, or $T = 0.6J$. Substituting $0.6J$ for T in the first equation gives $M=1.6(0.6J)$ or $M = 0.96J$. Thus Mary's income is 96 percent of Juan's income.

The correct answer is C.

45.

The lowest number of miles per gallon can be calculated using the lowest possible miles and the highest amount of gasoline. Also, the highest number of miles per gallon can be calculated using the highest possible miles and the lowest amount of gasoline.

Since the miles are rounded to the nearest 10 miles, the number of miles is between 285 and 295.

Since the gallons are rounded to the nearest gallon, the number of gallons is between 11.5 and 12.5. Therefore, the lowest number of miles per gallon is $\frac{lowest\ miles}{highest\ gallons} = \frac{285}{12.5}$ and the highest number of miles per gallon is $\frac{highest\ miles}{lowest\ gallons} = \frac{295}{11.5}$.

The correct answer is D.

46.

Let x be the average daily revue for the last 4 days. Using the formula $average = \frac{sum\ of\ values}{number\ of\ values}$, the information regarding the average revenues for the 10 day and 6 day periods can be expressed as follows and solved for x:

$$\$400 = \frac{6(\$360) + 4x}{10}$$

$\$4000 = 6(\$360)+4x$ Multiply both sides by 10

$\$1840 = 4x$ Subtract 6($360) from both sides

$\$460 = x$ Divide both sides by 4

The correct answer is D

47.

From this, the workers on the night crew will load $\frac{3}{4}\left(\frac{4}{5}\right) = \frac{3}{5}$ as many boxes as the day crew. The total loaded by both the day and night crews is thus $1 + \frac{3}{5} = \frac{8}{5}$ of the day crew's work. Therefore, the fraction of all boxes loaded by the two crews that was done by the day crew was $\frac{1}{\frac{8}{5}} = \frac{5}{8}$.

The correct answer is E.

48.

First calculate the actual total amount for the meal with a 10 percent tip and a 15 percent tip. To calculate each, multiply the cost of the meal by (1+ the percent as a decimal).

10 percent tip = 35.50 + 3.55 = 39.05

15 percent tip = 35.50 +3.55 + 1.775 = 40.825

Note that by splitting the 15 percent tip into a 10 percent and 5 percent tip you can potentially save a few seconds in calculation.

The only answer choice that includes all values between $39.05 and $40.83 is B.

The correct answer is B.

49.

This is a question which invites us to evaluate the answer choices and save some time. We can see immediately that the easiest number to deal with is answer choice D. But 50 x 12 = 600 so this answer is not possible. That said the next smallest answer must be the correct answer, as this number would allow a largest number of members to donate at least $12.

The correct answer is C.

50.

The lowest possible price is paid when the maximum initial discount of 40% is received.

$16(0.6) = $9.60   Calculate the first 40% discount

$9.60(0.75)= $7.20   Calculate the second 25% discount

The correct answer is B.

51.

Let J and B be Jack's and Bill's current ages. Then the information from the problem can be expressed in the following two equations:

$J = B + 14$, or equivalently $B = J - 14$ and $J + 10 = 2(B + 10)$.

Since Jack's age is to be determined, replace B in the second equation with $J - 14$ to get an equation that can be solved for J:

$J + 10 = 2(J - 14 + 10)$

$J + 10 = 2J - 8$

$18 = J$

Therefore, Jack's current age is 18, and hence Jack's age in 5 years will be $18 + 5 = 23$.

The correct answer is D.

52.

Don't waste time trying to work through the maths here in an overly complicated way.

If the pool takes 8 hours to fill 60% (or 3/5), then the remaining 40% will require:

$$\frac{8}{60}(40) = \frac{16}{3} = 5\frac{1}{3} = 5 \; hours \; and \; 20 \; minutes$$

The correct answer is B.

53.

Before the evaporation occurs, the tank contains 10,000 (0.05) = 500 gallons of sodium chloride. After the evaporation occurs, the tank contains 10,000 − 2,500 = 7,500 gallons of solution, of which 500 gallons are known to be sodium chloride. Calculate the percentage based on these post-evaporation amounts:

$$\frac{500}{7500} = 0.0667 = 6.67\%$$

The correct answer is D.

54.

Using the given ratios, the information about the fruits in the mixture can be expressed as $6x + 5x + 2x = 39$ or $13x = 39$ and thus $x = 3$. There are $6x$ or $6(3) = 18$ pounds of apples and $2x$ or $2(3) = 6$ pounds of grapes. Therefore, there are $18 - 6 = 12$ more pounds of apples than pounds of grapes in 39 pounds of the mixture.

The correct answer is B.

55.

Let G equal the number of games played by the team this season. The given information can be expressed as $(0.80)(100) + 0.50(G - 100) = 0.70G$, that is, 80 percent of the first 100 games plus 50 percent of the remaining games equals 70 percent of the total number of games played. This equation can be solved for G to determine the answer to the problem.

$(0.80)(100) + 0.50(G - 100) = 0.70G$

$80 + 0.50G - 50 =$	$0.70G$	Simplify and distribute
$30 =$	$0.20G$	Simplify and subtract $0.05G$ from both sides
$150 =$	G	Multiply by 5

The correct answer is D.

56.

According to the given information, 96 out of every 100 million vehicles were in an accident last year. Thus, of the 3 billion vehicles on the highway last year, the number of vehicles involved in accidents was:

$\frac{96}{100,000,000} \times 3,000,000,000$; cancel out all the zeroes which leaves us with

$\frac{96}{1} \times 30 = 2880 \; vehicles$

The correct answer is C.

57.

Another way of stating that a coin toss will turn up tails at least once is to say that it will not turn up heads every time. The probability that on at least one of the tosses the coin will not turn up heads is 1 minus the probability that the coin will turn up heads on all three tosses. Each toss is an independent event, and so the probability of getting heads all three times is $(\frac{1}{2})^2 = \frac{1}{8}$.

Thus the probability of not getting heads all three times (that is, getting tails at least once) is $1 - \frac{1}{8} = \frac{7}{8}$.

The correct answer is D.

58.

Both 3 to 4 and 6 to 8 are examples of two quantities in the ratio 3 to 4. Increasing both numbers in each of these examples by 5 gives 8 to 9 and 11 to 13. Since $\frac{8}{9} \neq \frac{11}{13}$, the ratio of the two new quantities cannot be determined from the information given.

The correct answer is E.

59.

Scanning the answer choices, it should be immediately clear that the only possible answers are A or B, given all the others are less than ½!

With each stroke's removal of ½ of the tank's air, the amount of air being removed from the tank on that stroke is equal to the amount of air remaining in the tank after that stroke.

Stroke	Air removed
1	½
2	¼
3	1/8
4	1/16

Thus the amount of air removed after 4 strokes is (converting all fractions to 16ths)

$$\frac{8+4+2+1}{16} = \frac{15}{16}$$

The correct answer is A.

60.

Let x be the total production of the past n days. Using the formula $average = \frac{sum\ of\ values}{number\ of\ values}$, the information in the problem can be expressed in the following two equations:

$50 = \frac{x}{n}$ Daily average of 50 units over the past n days

$55 = \frac{x+90}{n+1}$ Increased daily average when including today's 90 units

Solving the first equation for x gives $x = 50n$. Then substituting $50n$ for x in the second equation gives the following that can be solved for n:

$55 = \frac{50n + 90}{n + 1}$

$55\,(n + 1) = 50n + 90$ Multiply both sides by $(n + 1)$

$55n + 55 = 50n + 90$ Distribute the 55

$5n = 35$ Subtract $50n$ and 55 from both sides

$n = 7$ Divide both sides by 5

The correct answer is E.

61.

Let w represent the original hourly wage. Letting h be the original number of hours the employee worked per week, the original weekly income can be expressed as wh. Given a 25% increase in hourly wage, the employee's new wage is thus $1.25w$. Letting H be the reduced number of hours, the problem can then be expressed as:

$1.25wH = wh$ (new wage)(new hours) = (original wage)(original hours)

By dividing both sides by w, this equation can be solved for H.

$1.25H = h$

$H = 0.8h$

Since the new hours should be 0.8 = 80% of the original hours, the number of hours worked should be reduced by 20 percent.

The correct answer is B.

62.

The simple way to approach this question is to pick two numbers, one odd and one even, and test these numbers in each answer. Generally when picking numbers, choose small numbers which you can work with easily, but avoid picking 1 wherever possible.

If you pick 2 and 3 and test them in each answer, you'll find that only answer choice C produces two even answers.

The correct answer is C.

63.

Since 0.01ml evaporated every day, it follows that 0.2ml evaporated over 20 days.

Thus the percentage which evaporated is $\frac{0.2}{10} = \frac{2}{100} = 2\%$.

The correct answer is D.

64.

First determine the rate each machine produces widgets per second:

Machine A produces $\frac{120}{40} = 3 \ widgets/second$

Machine B produces $\frac{100}{20} = 5 \ widgets/second$

Thus we know that the two machines combined produce 8 widgets/second.

Finally, $\frac{200}{8} = 25$, thus the two machines combined will take 25s to produce 200 widgets.

The correct answer is B.

65.

The best way to solve this problem is to pick a small number which is greater than 6, such as 7 (Remember: Easy numbers to work with!) and then substitute it into each answer choice.

e.g.

A: $\frac{(7)(8)(3)}{3}$ We can cancel the 3 in the numerator and the 3 in the demoniator and determine that that this is divisible by 3.

This method initially eliminates answer choices C and D.

Next we choose another small integer (e.g. 8) and only apply this to the remaining three equations. This eliminates B and E.

The correct answer is A.

Practice Answers – Verbal

1.

Situation

Life expectancy in mid-nineteenth century North America was 40 years; now it is almost 80. What we think of as the prime of life must have been considered old in that earlier era.

Reasoning

What point weakens this argument? The argument is discussing life expectancy over the entire population of those born alive. The argument relies on the idea that if 40 years was the average life expectancy, then the usual length of life must have been around 40. But averages can be misleading. What if, in the nineteenth century, the number of infants born alive but not surviving their first year was far higher than it is today? If this were so, it would significantly reduce the *average age at time of death* of the population as a whole – but of course that population could have contained many who lived well into their seventies or eighties. Thus, if we add the information that first-year infant mortality was quite high 150 years ago, the conclusion that 40 years was considered old then would be much less well supported.

- A. The size of the population is irrelevant to the argument.
- B. **Correct.** Greatly reducing first-year infant mortality will have a large impact on the average life expectancy of the population as a whole. That, rather than grown adults living twice as long, is enough to account for a large portion of the doubling in average life expectancy.
- C. This point supports rather than weakens the argument.
- D. This point supports the argument.
- E. Exercise may have helped some nineteenth century people to live longer than they otherwise would. How many people – and what percentage of the population? Did this help them live past 40? If so, how long? If we had some of this information, it might affect the argument. But since this option does not provide these answers, it has little effect on the argument.

The correct answer is B.

2.

Situation

Adults aged 40 to 50 buy more ice cream than does any other demographic group (for example, teenagers). Does this mean that adults consume more ice cream than teenagers do?

Reasoning

A flawed assumption underlies the reason: the assumption that the buyers of the ice cream are also the eaters of the ice cream. Although the demographic group homeowners aged 40 to 50 purchases more ice cream than does any other demographic group, it is quite likely that much of the ice cream purchased by those homeowners is for consumption by family members rather than for exclusive consumption by the purchaser. This leaves open the possibility that teenagers may indeed be the largest consumers of ice cream.

- A. **Correct.** The failure to make this distinction let to the making of the flawed assumption.
- B. This is false: The argument tells us (indirectly) that homeowners aged 40 to 50 buy more ice cream than does any other group – which allows us to infer that they buy more than do homeowners aged 30 to 40, for example. But even if the argument had stated such information explicitly, it would not have offered any better support for its conclusion.
- C. There is nothing in the argument to suggest that the information given is based on popular belief.
- D. Providing precise information about the quantity of ice cream purchased by homeowners aged 40 to 50 would not improve the argument at all.
- E. The subject is ice cream, not nutrition, so this point is irrelevant.

The correct answer is A.

3.

Situation

In 1940, electricity was predicted to revolutionize agriculture. This prediction suggested that electric current running between electrodes inserted into the soil would kill bugs and weeds while encouraging the growth of crop plants.

Reasoning

Which point most suggests that the logic used in formulating the prediction is flawed? Electricity will revolutionize agriculture, it is said, because current can be run through electrodes placed in the soil. This current will kill bugs and weeds while strengthening plants. But how will the current accomplish this feat? More specifically, how will it kill one kind of plant (weeds) while strengthening another (crop plants)?

- A. The logic of the prediction has nothing to do with whether the current can be turned on and off; rather, it is concerned with the current itself and its effects.
- B. Rather than suggesting that the logic of the prediction is flawed, this serves to support the prediction: Farmers' saving on chemicals would be part of the predicted agricultural revolution.

C. The argument does not take for granted that the use of electricity is always beneficial; it merely suggests that it would be of great benefit to agriculture.
D. **Correct.** This statement properly identifies a problem with the prediction: It provides no reason to believe that the electricity would affect crop plants and weeds differently.
E. Rather than suggesting that the logic of the prediction is flawed, this serves to support the prediction: Changes in planting machines would be part of the predicted agricultural revolution.

The correct answer is D.

4.

A. An increase in expenditure on packing material and labour might affect the company's profitability, but it would have no effect on whether items were damaged in transit.
B. **Correct.** This statement adequately explains why more items, rather than fewer, were damaged in transit.
C. If customers were able to remove their items just as easily from boxes filled with more packing material as from boxes using less packing material, the items would be unaffected by an increase in the amount of packing material used.
D. The kind of goods TrueSave ships most frequently is not relevant to the question of why increasing the amount of packing material failed to reduce the number of items damaged in transit, since they most likely shipped this same kind of goods both before and after making the recommended change.
E. The loss of regular customers helps explain why TrueSave turned to the packaging consultants for help, but it does not help explain why those consultants' recommendation failed to reduce the number of items damaged in transit.

The correct answer is B.

5.

A. People who do not watch television are irrelevant to the argument.
B. The fact that cable television subscriptions include access to advertising-free public-television channels does not weaken the argument that "free" television is not free.
C. The picture quality of cable and free television are not at issue in this argument.
D. **Correct.** This statement properly identifies a factor that weakens the spokesperson's argument: If the cost of the advertising on "free" television is ultimately passed on to consumers in the prices they pay for the advertised product, and many cable channels have comparable amounts of advertising,

then cable television will necessarily have the same kind of hidden cost as "free" television.

E. Television viewers who do not watch cable channels have a choice as to which channels and programs they view. For example, they could watch channels with no advertising. So this information does not differentiate cable-television viewers from "free" television viewers.

The correct answer is D.

6.

Situation

Wood smoke is hazardous, so restrictive legislation is needed.

Reasoning

Which point supports the need for legislation? The argument for legislation is based on the position that wood smoke is hazardous to people's health. Any evidence of physical harm resulting from wood smoke supports the argument that legislation is needed. Undoubtedly, poor air quality caused by a high concentration of wood smoke presents just such a health risk.

- A. If wood smoke were as dangerous as car exhaust, this might support the idea of regulating it just as exhaust emissions are regulated; but this statement tells us it is less dangerous.
- B. This point suggests less of a need for legislation.
- C. This information provides no support for the idea that the use of wood-burning stoves should be regulated.
- D. The lack of benefit from banning open-air fires is a point against the legislation.
- **E. Correct.** This supports the argument in favour of legislation.

The correct answer is E.

7.

- **A. Correct.** This statement tells us that over the next ten years, a larger proportion of the population will probably be moviegoers and this could significantly increase movie attendance in Washington County.
- B. While stimulating downtown revitalization is a worthy goal, this does not help explain why more people would be likely to go to the movies in Washington County. Further, it raises the question of whether theatres in a revitalised downtown would draw business away from theatres in other locations, thus reducing the established cinema operators' profits.

C. This provides a reason to doubt the investors' prediction, because if spending on videos is increasing, people are probably less likely to see movies in movie theatres.
D. Regardless of how many screens each new cinema has relative to the established cinemas, none of them will be profitable if they cannot attract sufficient numbers of cinemagoers.
E. Cinemas' profitability depending on their sales of snacks and drinks does not explain why more people would go to the cinema in the first place.

The correct answer is A.

8.

A. This information seems to refer to recent changes in bats' habits – but the passage tells us that the fear being discussed is "long-standing". A long-standing fear cannot be adequately explained by recent changes.
B. The fact that bats provide a benefit for human beings does not explain human fear of them.
C. This tells us the fear is widespread but throws no light on what causes it.
D. **Correct.** This suggests that one of more factors other than bats' shyness and nocturnal habits are needed to explain humans' reactions to bats. For example, false beliefs about bats would be one such factor.
E. This suggests that more knowledge about the characteristics of some animal species may produce more, not less, fear. But this is quite compatible with the idea that lack of knowledge about the behaviour of bats could explain people's fearful reaction to them. One effect of lack of knowledge, for example, is allowing false beliefs to flourish.

The correct answer is D.

9.

Situation

The hunter claims that hunters have been identified by many people as the sole cause of the decline in Greenrock National Forest's deer population. But the hunter argues that black bears have also contributed to the deer population decline. Black bears are protected and have increased in number, and they have been found to have fed recently on deer.

Reasoning

What role in the argument is played by the hunter's statement that many people blame hunters alone for the decline in the national forest's deer population? In this statement, the hunter claims that many people have judged hunters responsible for the decline.

The hunter then goes on to offer evidence supporting a different judgment: that hunters are *not* solely responsible, but that black bears are also to blame.

   A. The hunter's main conclusion is that black bears have also contributed to the decline in the deer population.
   B. The argument seeks to offer a reason for the finding that the deer population has declined, not the finding that people blame hunters for that decline.
   C. The hunter does not conclude that blaming hunters for the decline in the deer population is correct; rather, the hunter suggests that black bears should also be blamed.
   D. The hunter believes that hunters are *not* solely responsible for the decline in the deer population, so people's suggestion that they *are* responsible does not support the hunter's main conclusion.
   E. **Correct.** The boldfaced statement cites a judgment that the hunter attributes to many people, and that the hunter argues is incorrect. The hunter opposes the judgment that hunters alone are responsible for the decline in the deer population.

The correct answer is E.

10.

   A. Falling prices and falling demand do not explain the falling productivity of the trees.
   B. The lack of pests and diseases among imported trees does not explain the sharply decreased productivity.
   C. **Correct.** If there are fewer fruit-producing female flowers, there is likely to be less fruit.
   D. If the weevil population pollinating the trees remained the same, one would expect that productivity would have remained the same, rather than declining. So this cannot provide an adequate explanation.
   E. This information is unlikely to be relevant to the change that occurred in 1984.

The correct answer is C.

11.

   A. The patient's argument has to do with whether the physician's refusal to prescribe synthetic melatonin is consistent with the physician's usual prescription practices. The question of whether naturally produced melatonin has different side effects than synthetic melatonin has no bearing on that argument.
   B. It is quite reasonable for the patient's argument not to mention this possibility, especially since the physician expresses a belief that synthetic

melatonin may be effective – but expresses no belief about whether or not it has been conclusively shown to be effective.
C. Awareness that sleep disorders can lead to serious medical complications most likely prompts the patient's desire for treatment – but the patient's not mentioning this possible consequence of sleep disorders does not indicate a flaw in the argument.
D. The patient makes clear that the physician prescribes medications that have serious side effects; the time those side effects take to manifest themselves is not relevant to the argument.
E. **Correct.** The patient's argument is flawed in failing to consider this key difference between known risks and unknown risks. If the patient had considered this key difference the patient would have realised that the physician's position is not at all inconsistent, and that the physician's refusal to prescribe is genuinely based on a concern about an unknown risk.

The correct answer is E.

12.

A. The greater number of similarities than differences in style in one population could be attributed to either cultural acquisition or genetic transmission, so the conclusion is not strengthened.
B. **Correct.** Compared with the other options, this information provides the most additional support for the researchers' conclusion.
C. The cited differences are among populations of the same species; differences between species are outside the scope of the conclusion.
D. Since no information is given about the nest-building styles of these populations (whether or not they are of the same species), the fact that they have little contact neither strengthens nor weakens the conclusion.
E. This statement provides an example of learned bird behaviour, and so provides a little additional support for the conclusion, but not as much additional support as does (B)

The correct answer is B.

13.

A. The method of the drug's distribution is irrelevant, unless the central authority can limit the drug's production from the bark of wild ibora trees. But this information is not provided.
B. The cost of producing the drug does not affect the outcome for the tree unless it deters production.
C. The existence of uses for other parts of the tree opens the possibility that the ibora-bark drug would cause no increase in destruction of trees other than what exists already. If this information were provided, it would weaken

support for the conclusion. Since it is not provided, this option does not significantly weaken the argument.
D. **Correct.** This information most weakens the argument.
E. Difficulty of access to the trees could provide a disincentive to their harvesting – but we are not told that it would prevent their harvesting.

The correct answer is D.

14.

A. **Correct.** This information strengthens the argument more than the information in any of the information in any of the other options.
B. This statement explains that some who eat fortified cereal sometimes omit other foods from their diet. But this bit of sociological information is irrelevant to the scientific issue of which type of breakfast is a better source of vitamins.
C. This statement provides an answer to the question "Why are some foods fortified with vitamins?" It does not address the question at issue, "Which type of breakfast is a better source of vitamins?"
D. This information is not evidence that a well-balanced breakfast is a better source of certain vitamins than is fortified cereal alone.
E. This information tells us that fortified cereal is not especially hard to digest – but does not indicate that a breakfast of fortified cereal alone is an inferior source of vitamins.

The correct answer is A.

15.

A. This statement makes a judgment that is explicitly contradicted in the passage, which states that an inconclusive polygraph result *is no reflection on the examinee.*
B. This sweeping conclusion is not as well supported by the passage as is (C). The passage discusses only inconclusive polygraph results.
C. **Correct.** Given the information in the passage, one can infer that inconclusive polygraph tests are sometimes used unfairly against job applicants – if one makes the reasonable assumption that judging a job applicant unsuitable is unfair if the judgment is based merely on the failure of a particular technique to provide reliable evidence.
D. The passage is concerned only with inconclusive tests, not cases when the polygraph test is mistaken.
E. Information about employers who do not consider polygraph tests is irrelevant to the discussion.

16.

The correct answer is C.

- A. The argument concerns innovation in bicycle technology. It is not about the entire market for all bicycles, so this claim about traditional bicycles is not assumed.
- B. The passage does not discuss where the best innovations are likely to be created, so no assumption about small workshops versus large manufacturers is made.
- C. **Correct.** This statement identifies information that appropriately fills the gap in the reasoning as stated in the passage.
- D. This claim provides an explanation of manufacturers' technological conservatism that is quite different from the explanation indicated in the passage.
- E. The passage does not indicate what the racing authorities do or do not know about bicycle innovation – even though it suggests that they may be reluctant to approve every possible innovation for racing purposes.

The correct answer is C.

17.

- A. The information is about percentages, not total dollars; the percentages could have remained the same for each of three years even though sales income increased each year.
- B. There is no information about the competition faced by either division; the higher profit margin for the pharmaceutical division would suggest, if anything, less intense competition in its markets.
- C. **Correct.** If the information in the passage is true, then this must also be true.
- D. Since there is no information about the product mix, no inference about it is possible.
- E. The passage does not distinguish between highly profitable products and other products, so this inference cannot be drawn from the information.

The correct answer is C.

18.

- A. That other animals are fed the potentially contaminated feed is not relevant to the question of whether chickens are immune to the virus.
- B. The idea that there could be a source of the virus other than contaminated feed does not have any bearing on whether chickens are immune to the virus.
- C. The idea that there is a way for animals to acquire a resistance to the virus that causes Ferber's syndrome suggests that some animals, possibly chickens, might be immune to the virus. This is the opposite of what the argument is trying to establish.

D. **Correct.** This statement properly identifies a point that logically completes the argument. It provides a reason why infected chickens would fail to show symptoms of Ferber's syndrome.
E. If chickens' diets contain proportionally more of infected feed that cattles' diets do, it is even more surprising that Ferber's syndrome is not observed in chickens – far from providing a reason not to conclude that chickens are immune to the virus; this makes it seem even more likely that they are immune.

The correct answer is D.

19.

A. As long as the sample was representative, the figures should be accurate. This point does not weaken the conclusion.
B. **Correct.** This statement suggests that the 1.2 percent inflation rate is an unusual occurrence in recent years. Especially because the dip below the stable 4 percent rate was *temporary,* this unusual occurrence cannot be used as the basis for predicting a trend.
C. This statement explains one process by which inflation increases and tends to support the conclusion that inflation will continue to rise.
D. This information implies, for example, that two years ago, the inflation rate was higher than 1.2 percent. This raises the possibility (without stating it) that last year and the year preceding mark a trend of declining inflation (and that the current year's 4 percent is an aberration). However, if the inflation rate two years ago was only slightly higher than 1.2 percent (for example, 1.25 percent), then it would be difficult to regard these two numbers as signalling a trend of declining inflation. We do not have enough information here to regard this as a significant weakener. The information is sufficient to justify a little doubt about the argument's conclusion – but not at all specific enough to undermine the argument's conclusion as much as does (B).
E. The failure of government intervention to affect the rate of inflation could be seen to support, not weaken, the conclusion.

The correct answer is B.

20.

A. **Correct.** The addition of this information to the argument would weaken the argument more than would the information in any of the other options.
B. The more serious nature of the oil spills caused by tankers strengthens the argument.
C. Careful management controlling the environmental impact of offshore operations supports the argument rather than weakens it.

D. While offshore operations may cause other environmental damage, this point is not relevant to the argument, which concerns just oil spills.
E. Importing oil on tankers may be an attractive economic alternative, but because this point is unrelated to oil spills, it does not weaken the argument.

The correct answer is A.

21.

A. This point merely tells us how much coffee consumption has decreased; it does not make the explanation offered in the conclusion any less likely to be correct.
B. Withdrawal symptoms would occur only after decreased consumption has occurred and so cannot explain why the decrease occurred.
C. Suppose that the specialty coffees that had their sales hold steady were all caffeine-free coffees; note that nothing rules this out. If this were the case, the explanation would remain plausible.
D. An increase in the consumption of these drinks could plausibly be the result of some coffee drinkers switching to these drinks to avoid the negative effects of caffeine.
E. **Correct.** This statement properly identifies a plausible alternative explanation and therefore undermines the given explanation.

The correct answer is E.

22.

A. While this supports the idea that the Transit Authority can economically increase the number of train trips, it provides no information about whether the trains will be crowded.
B. Increasing the number of bus trips on routes that connect to subways would be likely to lead to more people to ride the subways. This makes it less likely that the officials' prediction – that delays due to overcrowding will not increase – will turn out to have been accurate.
C. This suggests that subway ridership will remain high, and thus that delays caused by overcrowding will continue.
D. **Correct.** This statement properly identifies a situation in which the officials' prediction is likely to turn out to have been accurate. The ridership will be increasing during times when more passengers will not create delays, since they will merely fill empty seats on existing trains.
E. While this supports the idea that the Transit Authority can economically increase the number of train trips, it provides no information about whether the trains will be crowded.

The correct answer is D.

23.

- A. The relative costs of the two options indicate nothing about whether by installing scrubbers the company will have done the most it can to reduce harmful emissions.
- B. Even if the company installs the most efficient scrubbers, it may be that there is more that Northern Power could do to reduce harmful emissions.
- C. Even if the company is fully committed to reducing harmful emissions, it could be that installing scrubbers is the most it can do to reduce harmful emissions.
- D. **Correct.** If harmful emissions could be reduced even more by using both methods, then installing scrubbers alone will not be the most that the company can do to reduce harmful emissions.
- E. Even if this were not assumed and the company's other activities did cause significant air pollution, it could still be that installing scrubbers is the most that the company can do to reduce harmful emissions *from its plants*; perhaps any of its other activities that do cause significant air pollution have nothing to do with its plants – for example, pollution coming from trucks the company uses.

The correct answer is D.

24.

- A. **Correct.** This statement properly identifies the factor that weakens the argument: A comparison could well be a valuable source of understanding if all foraging societies are shown to share certain features not found in other societies.
- B. This point slightly strengthens, rather than weakens, the argument.
- C. This point does not address the issue of comparing a modern society to an ancient society.
- D. The reason for this could be that these anthropologists know that such a comparison is not useful; thus this point does not weaken the argument.
- E. This point strengthens, rather than weakens, the argument.

The correct answer is A.

25.

- A. Even though the fee may indirectly have this effect, the argument need not assume that it will; perhaps residents will continue to buy as much but will make longer use of the product, or recycle it.
- B. The argument would be stronger if this were assumed NOT to be true.
- C. **Correct.** This statement properly identifies the fact that the argument rests on the assumption that the fee will not create illegal dumping.

D. The argument need not assume this, and nothing in the argument indicates that it does. Financial incentives could be enough to make the desired outcome happen even if residents are indifferent to the parkland's beauty.
E. The argument assumes that residents will reduce the amount of trash that they create, not that they will find other places to dispose of it.

The correct answer is C.

26.

A. This need not be assumed. The argument is not committed to any claim about the effects that watching television or listening to music may have on the development of communication skills in children.
B. The argument is limited to after-school hours or spare time.
C. **Correct.** This statement properly identifies the assumption on which the argument is based.
D. This could be false and the argument could still be sound; perhaps children who spend all their spare time playing computer games receive no formal instruction.
E. This could be false and the argument could still be sound as long as the intellectual development the games contribute to does not contribute to the development of communication skills.

The correct answer is C.

27.

A. Non-biodegradable plastic containers can be crushed completely flat. To say that biodegradable ones can be completely crushed also is perfectly compatible with saying that they contain less plastic.
B. **Correct.** This statement properly identifies a point that strengthens the argument by saying that the container actually produces more plastic refuse.
C. Consumers' preferences are not relevant to the argument about residual plastic.
D. The argument is not concerned with waste from manufacturing processes, but only with the product itself.
E. No reason is given to indicate that the inability to reuse the plastic from either type of container is related to the amount of plastic in either container.

The correct answer is B.

28.

A. If genetic factors accounted for such people's lack of increase of blood pressure with age, then their blood pressure would not increase when they moved to cities and adopted high salt diets.

- B. If people who eat high salt diets tend to have high blood pressure, it would support the idea that salt is indeed the culprit in high blood pressure.
- C. The argument is concerned with what happens when people from rain forest communities move to cities *and adopt high salt diets,* so the fact that it is possible to have a low salt diet in a city is not relevant.
- D. **Correct.** This statement properly identifies a reason why salt might not be responsible for high blood pressure: there could be some other dietary factor that, when adopted, causes high blood pressure.
- E. The argument is concerned with the effects of high salt diets. The fact that consuming too little salt can cause death says nothing about whether consuming too much salt is harmful.

The correct answer is D.

29.

- A. The same may be true of books and articles.
- B. This point does not indicate whether educational software is more comparable to inventions or to books and articles.
- C. This point could be true even if, with regard to the relevant criteria, educational software is more comparable to inventions than to books and articles.
- D. This point does not indicate whether educational software is more comparable to inventions or to books and articles.
- E. **Correct.** This statement properly identifies a premise that establishes the relationship required to complete the argument.

The correct answer is E.

30.

- A. This gives a reason why juvenile horseshoe crabs that do not burrow *would* have significant barnacle populations.
- B. If barnacles in areas of weak tidal currents readily attach themselves to horseshoe crabs, then it would be more likely for juvenile horseshoe crabs in such areas to have significant barnacle populations.
- C. The areas under discussion are those where tidal currents are very weak. The strength of currents may vary widely there, but presumably they are still weak compared to other areas.
- D. The surprising finding under discussion is why certain juvenile horseshoe crabs do not have significant barnacle populations, despite failing to engage in behaviour that dislodges barnacles. That a very large barnacle population can hurt a horseshoe crab does not help explain such a finding.
- E. **Correct.** This statement properly identifies something that helps explain the surprising finding: If juvenile horseshoe crabs regularly shed their shells,

they also regularly shed the barnacles that cling to those shells. Thus juvenile horseshoe crabs would most likely be found not to have significant barnacle populations.

The correct answer is E.

31.

- A. The issue is not about a similarity of symptoms but about where the parasites reside.
- B. The existence of malaria-free regions is not in question.
- C. The argument gives no reason to postulate any significant connection between the discontinuation of medication and the issue of whether symptoms can persist after a patient has been in a malaria-free region for 120 days.
- D. **Correct.** This statement properly identifies a point that weakens the conclusion.
- E. This tells us only that some individuals are immune; it does not help us determine whether those who are not can have symptoms occur more than 120 days after moving into a malaria-free area.

The correct answer is D.

32.

- A. This indicates one of the consequences of drought, and slightly suggests that this might be due to a lower algae level. But it does nothing to explain why algae levels might be lower after a drought.
- B. This could explain why some rivers that are slow-moving and have little water might have a high algae level – but not why the algae level is low in such rivers after a period of drought.
- C. This explains why levels of other species might be low when algae population are high, not why algae populations are high when there is little rain, but low following a period of extreme drought.
- D. **Correct.** This statement properly identifies something that helps explain the contrast. According to the information given, the habitat of the algae under discussion is river water. If the river dries up, the algae will probably not survive. Then after the drought, algae population levels would likely take a while to rise again.
- E. This emphasizes that there is a contrast between what happens to algae during periods of extreme drought and what happens to them at other times, but it does not help explain that contrast.

The correct answer is D.

33.

- A. The existence of vessels made both before and after A.D. 365 suggests that Kourion was not destroyed by the earthquake.
- B. **Correct.** This statement properly identifies evidence that supports the archaeologists' hypothesis.
- C. The occurrence of the earthquake is not in question; this statement simply confirms a fact already assumed in the argument.
- D. The existence of statues carved in styles current after the date of the earthquake (A.D. 365-A.D. 400) argues against the town's destruction in A.D. 365.
- E. The existence of inscriptions using an alphabet common only after the earthquake argues against the theory that the earthquake destroyed Kourion.

The correct answer is B.

34.

- A. In an indirect way, this option slightly weakens rather than strengthens the argument. For *if* fossil fuels are used to produce the electricity now used by the industries and *if* it is because of these newer technologies that output has increased, the argument's conclusion is *less* likely.
- B. It does not matter how much fossil fuel was used to manufacture the older technologies *originally.* That has no bearing on whether more fossil fuel was used to manufacture the older technologies *originally.* That has no bearing no whether more fossil fuel would have been expended as a result of the *continued operation* of the industries if the partial switch to newer technologies had not occurred.
- C. This is what we would expect, but it in no way strengthens the argument.
- D. This may seem to weaken the argument by indicating that the switch from older technologies will have less of an impact on fossil fuel consumption by these industries than we might have assumed. But since the conclusion makes no claim about how much consumption has been reduced, it is not clear that this option has any bearing on the strength of the argument one way or the other.
- E. **Correct.** This is the option that most strengthens the argument.

The correct answer is E.

35.

- A. Sharon's argument is about a normal level of unemployment; how rarely or frequently that level is exceeded is outside the scope of her argument.
- B. **Correct.** This statement properly identifies an assumption that underlies Sharon's argument.

C. Although Sharon's argument is compatible with saying that even more than 90 percent of the population knows someone who is unemployed, nothing suggests that she assumes that this is true.
D. Sharon's argument is not based on the figure Roland cites and does not assume its accuracy or inaccuracy; her argument merely points out that his figure is not inconsistent with a normal rate of unemployment.
E. The fear of losing a job is not part of Sharon's argument; this statement is irrelevant.

The correct answer is B.

36.

A. The greater ease of changing from the standard keyboard to the EFCO keyboard for typists experienced in both would support, not weaken, the conclusion.
B. The fewer repairs required by EFCO keyboards should save money in the long run; immediate costs will not go up since the price of both keyboards is the same. The conclusion is not weakened.
C. The increasing use of EFCO keyboards supports the conclusion, because it suggests that other offices have found the switch advantageous.
D. **Correct.** This statement properly identifies information that weakens the conclusion that savings will be immediate.
E. For new typists, training time is the same for both keyboards; this statement does not weaken the conclusion.

The correct answer is D.

37.

A. This weakly suggests that the overly centralized economy of Country X is to blame for its poor agricultural production; this strengthens the argument more than it weakens it.
B. The availability of a seaport does not explain the differences in agricultural production.
C. Similar climate conditions have already been established in the argument.
D. **Correct.** This statement properly identifies a factor that weakens the argument.
E. The government's intention when instituting the economy does not have any bearing on whether the economy is responsible for the decline or not.

The correct answer is D.

38.

A. This argument is not about how problems should be solved, only about how chief executives learn of them.
B. No recommendation for solving the problem is assumed; only the method of discovering the problem is assumed.
C. Problem-solving ability plays no role in the argument.
D. Correct. This statement properly identifies an assumption that underlies the argument.
E. This statement undermines the assertion made in the first sentence of the passage and so cannot be assumed.

The correct answer is D.

39.

A. While this statement about being ticketed may be true, the conclusion pertains to the recurrent exceeding of the speed limit, so this statement is not relevant.
B. Correct. This statement properly identifies the conclusion's necessary assumption about ticketed drivers' being more likely to drive in excess of the speed limit than nonticketed drivers.
C. This statement is about the number of vehicles ticketed, not about the regular habits of drivers, so it is not assumed for the conclusion
D. While the additional information could help support the conclusion, it is not a necessary assumption in the conclusion because it is about the particular example of the drivers in Maryland, not about drivers' habits in general.
E. Learning that Maryland drivers are not representative of other drivers undermines the conclusion about all drivers, so it is clearly not assumed.

The correct answer is B.

40.

A. If employers consented to employees' request and diverted money from safety to wages, this statement might cast doubt on the conclusion. However, no such reallocation of resources is implied, and the passage conclusively states that more money *is* spent on safety precautions and machinery maintenance when demand for the product is high. Therefore this statement is irrelevant.
B. **Correct.** This statement properly identifies a point that undermines the conclusion.
C. Increased job security could result in an increased number of workers, which might increase the total number of accidents. However, the conclusion is about the number of accidents *per employee,* so this point is irrelevant.
D. Actively promoting safety with an award would tend to support the argument, not weaken it.

E. Replacing outdated machinery with more modern machinery could result in a safer workplace; this point could strengthen the conclusion.

The correct answer is B.

41.

A. This statement rules out the possibility that submitted articles were not published, and eliminating this alternate explanation tends to support the argument.
B. A decline in waiting time would seem to promote more articles about accelerator research being written and published, not fewer.
C. While the decline in articles could be explained by a decline in the number of journals, this statement eliminates that alternate explanation.
D. If the accelerators can be used for multiple experiments, then it is reasonable to expect more articles related to them, not fewer.
E. **Correct.** This statement properly identifies a point that undermines the journalist's reasoning.

The correct answer is E.

42.

A. The argument does not require this because the conclusion does not address allergic reactions to substances other than sulfites.
B. The argument specifically refers to 'certain sulfites' producing allergic reactions. It is entirely compatible with certain other forms of sulfites not producing allergic reactions in anyone.
C. This is irrelevant. The argument does not claim that one can avoid having an allergic reation to sulfites *from any source* just by restricting one's wine consumption to those varieties to which no sulfites have been added.
D. Once again, the argument's conclusion does not address allergic reactions to substances other than sulfites in wine.
E. **Correct.** The argument relies on this assumption.

The correct answer is E.

43.

A. The evidence of the blood vessels in the wings does not conflict with other evidence.
B. The evidence of the blood vessels in the wings is used to support only one theory – that Sandactylus flew by flapping its wings as well as by gliding; no evidence is discussed in relation to any earlier theory.

- C. **Correct.** This statement properly identifies how the argument compares the wings of bats of the Sandactylus in order to draw a conclusion about how the dinosaur flew.
- D. The argument is not about how the structures in the bats developed from the structures in the dinosaurs, but rather about how Sandactylus flew.
- E. The comparison between bats and Sandactylus points out similarities, not differences.

The correct answer is C.

44.

- A. This has no obvious bearing on the argument one way or another. It makes it more likely, perhaps, that a person in a distant state will retire to Florida, but less likely that one in a neighbouring state will do so.
- B. This has no bearing whether fewer people have been retiring to Florida over the last ten years.
- C. **Correct.** This is the option that most seriously weakens the argument.
- D. This makes it *more* likely that Florida's economy will be harmed because of decreasing numbers of retirees, but has no real bearing on the argument which concludes specifically that *declines in the proportion of emigrating retirees moving to Florida* will have a negative effect on the state's economy.
- E. This is irrelevant. At issue is how the numbers of retirees in Florida from one year compare to the next, not how those numbers compare with numbers of retirees in other states.

The correct answer is C.

45.

- A. Although the environmentalist claims that technology cause people' s greater encroachment on nature in this single instance, there is nothing in the argument to suggest that such encroachment caused by technology is a general trend.
- B. The environmentalist's claims imply that the number of fish caught is not a reliable indicator of how many are left in the ocean but do not give any indication that it is possible to find out by any other means either.
- C. The environmentalist creates an analogy between fish caught and rainforest trees cut down but does not compare their proportion.
- D. Nothing about how the fish can be used, including whether they are edible or inedible, plays any role in the environmentalist's argument.
- E. **Correct.** This statement properly identifies a conclusion supported by the environmentalist's statement: The marine fish are endangered.

The correct answer is E.

46.

    A. The fact that the absolute amount of credit that was extended to retailers went up in the second year does not help to explain why the *proportion that was paid on time* also went up.
    B. If anything, this would suggest that more retailers would have trouble paying their credit to wholesalers on time.
    C. **Correct.** This is the option that most helps to explain the phenomenon.
    D. Just because retailers *tried* to stimulate sales does not mean that they succeeded, and the passage tells us that the downturn in sales in the clothing trade continued into the second year.
    E. This does not change the fact that there was a downturn in sales of clothing during the first year. Furthermore, the question is why the rate of unpaid credit dropped in the *second* year of the recession.

The correct answer is C.

47.

    A. The argument does not assume that no country acts according to the theory, just that not all countries do so.
    B. The commentator's argument is about what the theory of trade retaliation predicts, not about what trade policies countries ought to follow, and a statement about the latter is not an assumption for the former.
    C. This alternative scenario – trade disputes settled by international tribunal rather than by trade retaliation – plays no role in the argument.
    D. **Correct.** This statement properly identifies the assumption required to create the never ending action reaction pattern.
    E. The argument does not pertain to countries' initial reasons for closing their markets to foreign trade, only to the consequences of doing so.

The correct answer is D.

48.

    A. This undermines the psychologists' interpretation, for it shows that the same phenomenon occurs even when the alleged cause has been removed.
    B. **Correct.** This option identifies the result that would most strengthen the psychologists' interpretation.
    C. This undermines the psychologists' interpretation by showing that the same phenomenon occurs even when the alleged cause has been removed; patrons cannot be reminded of something that is not there.
    D. To the extent that this bears on the interpretation of the study, it weakens it. Patrons *using* credit cards are surely aware that they credit and yet they spend *less* generously.

- E. This does not support the idea that being reminded that one has a credit card induces one to be *more generous*, only that it induces one to *use* that credit card.

The correct answer is B.

49.

- A. This might make the assurance of the proponents less credible but it does not make their claim misleading.
- B. Nothing about the proponents' claim suggests that the only effect irradiation has is to kill bacteria.
- C. The fact that cooking and irradiation have different purposes does not indicate that the proponents' claim suggests something that is false.
- D. If anything, this strengthens the proponents' point by minimizing the relative damage caused by irradiation.
- E. **Correct.** This option most logically completes the argument.

The correct answer is E.

50.

- A. Although international discord would likely result from a blockade, no information allows a conclusion to be drawn about the balance of opinion.
- B. This conclusion is not justified because a successful embargo requires both international accord and the ability to enforce the embargo.
- C. This statement simply defines the purpose of a blockade; it is not a conclusion from the information given.
- D. **Correct.** This statement properly identifies a conclusion supported by the claims.
- E. The necessary condition for success is *a high degree of international accord*, not unanimity, so this conclusion cannot be justified.

The correct answer is D.

51.

- A. Lower labour costs may explain the lower production costs in Country Q, but there may be a variety of other reasons as well.
- B. It is possible that manufacturing jobs would be decreased, but no evidence in the passage leads that conclusion.
- C. **Correct.** This statement properly identifies the point that, for importing to be less expensive, tariffs and transportation costs together must be less than 10 percent of manufacturing cost, therefore, tariffs alone must be less than 10 percent.

D. If transportation costs were more than 10 percent, importing would be more expensive, not less.
E. Less production time may explain the lower costs in Country Q, but there may be a variety of other reasons as well.

The correct answer is C.

52.

A. The fact that Colson's may be seeing fewer customers does not mean that the discount stores that close will not be replaced by stores that in no way compete with Colson's or SpendLess.
B. **Correct.** This option most seriously weakens the argument.
C. If anything, this strengthens the argument by indication that Goreville's central shopping district is thriving.
D. This, too, strengthens the argument because one is more likely to open a new store in an area with a growing population.
E. Because this statement does not indicate whether any of these stores that offer goods not sold at SpendLess or Colson's will be among those that are closing, it is not possible to determine what effect it has on the strength of the argument.

The correct answer is B.

53.

A. The passage does not say that weight is the sole measure of development; this statement fails to point out any error in the reasoning.
B. The greater weight of some infants would be calculated in reaching the average.
C. This birth weight may be consistent with the weight range at three months; not enough information is provided to make a judgment.
D. The passage does not claim that *below average* is the same as *insufficient* so pointing out the distinction does not show an error in the reasoning.
E. **Correct.** This statement properly identifies the logical flaw in the reasoning, which takes evidence about average weight to draw a conclusion about average weight gain. The two measures are not the same.

The correct answer is E.

54.

A. **Correct.** This option provides the most support for the claim.
B. This may provide a reason for supporting the proposal, but it provides no support for either (1) or (2).

C. This indicates that it is better to receive fire calls from telephones than from alarm boxes – other things being equal but that supports neither (1) or (2). There is still the possibility that the only person aware that a fire has started is near an alarm box but lacks access to a telephone.
D. This merely indicates that it would be good if the proposal had the intended effects.
E. This actually *weakens* support for (2), by enhancing the possibility that the only person aware that a fire has started is near an alarm box but lacks access to a working telephone.

The correct answer is A.

55.

A. The method of guidance is irrelevant to the argument about fee wheel versus fixed linear systems.
B. The passage compares the speed and system models of airplanes and high speed trains. The argument does not incorporate buses and cars, which are included only to give examples of free wheel systems, and so this statement is irrelevant.
C. **Correct.** This statement properly identifies the weakness in the argument: Airplanes are not truly a free wheel system because they are restricted to traveling between airports. Additionally, airports tend to be less conveniently located than train terminals, which has further potential to weaken the argument in favour of airplanes.
D. The inability of high speed trains to use some convenient train stations strengthens, rather than weakens, the argument in favour of airplanes.
E. Consumer preference for air travel over ground travel on long trips strengthens, rather than weakens, the argument in favour of airplanes.

The correct answer is C.

56.

A. The argument does not rely on any information about the number of television assemblers in Vernland nor for that matter on the number of TVs assembled in Vernland.
B. The argument need not assume there is any difference in the features of the TVs produced in the two countries. Increased sales of Vernland TVs in Bofodia could be due to any number of other reasons, such as price or quality.
C. **Correct.** This option states an assumption on which the argument depends.
D. The argument does not depend upon this being so: Vernland's domestic TV sales (or perhaps its exports to countries other than Borodia) may have decreased by more than its imports into Borodia have increased.

E. The argument's conclusion addresses what *has* happened; the argument in no way relies on any assumptions about what may or may not happen in the coming years.

The correct answer is C.

57.

A. This option applies equally to both eras, so it has no bearing on the argument.
B. It is not clear whether carpenters working on larger hotels would exercise more, less, or the same skill and care as those working on smaller hotels; thus this option does not weaken the argument.
C. The argument does not rely, even implicitly, on there being any difference in the quality of materials used in the two eras, so it does not weaken the argument to point out that no such difference exists.
D. **Correct.** This weakens the reasoning in the argument by showing a respect in which the comparison between *existing* hotels in unrepresentative.
E. The longer a carpenter works as an apprentice, the more skill he or she is apt to have upon becoming a full-fledged carpenter. So this option would tend to slightly strengthen rather than weaken the argument.

The correct answer is D.

58.

A. The ability to schedule direct flights would be an advantage, not a disadvantage.
B. The decline in the price of aviation fuel might make the plan seem less pressing, and it could conceivably complicate the issue of whether the expected savings would justify the investment in new planes. However, lower fuel costs would not diminish the crucial time saving advantage of Skybuses, and any hypotheses about their relevance to the overall decision are purely speculative.
C. The ability to eliminate refuelling is an advantage to the airline. The loss of jobs could, in theory, have some negative effect on the airline due to lowered morale among remaining employees. However *several* does not support a hypothesis that the effect would be very significant, and any hypotheses about whether it might override the benefits are purely speculative.
D. The decisions made by other airlines are irrelevant to the plan.
E. **Correct.** This statement properly identifies a potentially serious disadvantage to the plan.

The correct answer is E.

59.

A. To the extent that risk of bodily harm decreases longevity, this weakens rather than strengthens the argument.
B. This option, too, weakens the argument rather than strengthens it, since it suggests that marriage does indeed enhance one's longevity.
C. Even if a person with unhealthy habits who marries is more likely to wind up with a spouse with unhealthy habits than is a person with healthy habits who marries, that tells us nothing about whether the average person who gets married gets a boot in longevity.
D. This option does not tell us whether it is also true of those who never marry that most of them who give up an unhealthy habit as a young adult ever resume that habit later in life. Thus, by itself, this option has no bearing on the strength of the argument.
E. Correct. This strengthens the argument against the causal connection between marriage and longevity by showing that the longevity difference disappears when the longevity of those who marry young is compared with young adults with similar health habits who will never marry.

The correct answer is E.

60.

A. The argument does not suggest that the Mayans used ceramics for implements, so this point does not weaken the argument; it is irrelevant to it.
B. Since the point of the argument is who, specifically, established a settlement to Colha 4,500 years ago, the evidence that some unidentified people were practicing agriculture there at that time neither strengthens nor weakens the argument.
C. Discovering how the implements were used does not explain who was using them, so this information is not relevant to the conclusion.
D. **Correct.** This statement properly identifies the weakness in the argument that the similarity between the 4,500 year old implements and the later Mayan implements may be attributed to the Mayans' adopting the style of implements used earlier by another culture.
E. That the Mayans relied on agricultural symbols at that time is nearly irrelevant to the issue of whether the earlier implements belonged to their culture. To the extent that this is relevant, it very slightly supports, rather than weakens, the argument; *highly developed* suggests that Mayans had been practicing.

The correct answer is D.

61.

A. Examples of the copyists' handwriting might help date Codex Berinensis; the absence of handwriting samples does not help support 1148 as the date.

B. The length of the plague, while it may account for the succession of copyists, does not help support the particular year the work was done.
C. The amount of work a copyists could achieve each day does not provide any information about the year the work appeared.
D. **Correct.** This statement properly identifies a circumstance that supports the hypothesis.
E. The productivity or tenure of the various copyists is irrelevant to establishing the date.

The correct answer is D.

62.

A. To the extent that this is even relevant, it tends to weaken the hypothesis; it makes less likely the possibility that Neanderthals used other types of musical instruments employing the diatonic scale.
B. This also weakens the hypothesis, because it states that there is no known evidence of a certain type that would support the hypothesis.
C. The fact that the cave-bear bone fragment that was apparently a flute came from a site where many other cave-bear skeletal remains were found has little bearing on the hypothesis, and in no way supports it.
D. This does not strengthen the hypothesis, for even if the option were falsi – even if a simpler instrument could be constructed that employed the diatonic scale – the existence of a flute employing the diatonic scale would provide no less support for the hypothesis.
E. **Correct.** This option most strongly supports the hypothesis.

The correct answer is E.

63.

A. This would strengthen the argument since the pricing competition among independent suppliers is an advantage for the company.
B. **Correct.** The statement properly identifies one disadvantage of outsourcing: the company no longer controls access to its information and plans. With the increased possibility of competitors' gaining access to its proprietary information, the company's business is put at risk.
C. Providing examples of the tasks typically outsourced or handled internally does not affect the argument.
D. Expertise in a particular area is an advantage of outsourcing and thus a strength of the argument.
E. The supplier's hiring of members of the company's staff to handle work no longer performed within the company is not shown to be a disadvantage.

The correct answer is B.

64.

- A. The destination of the object after its creation is not the issue.
- B. The extent to which some cabinetmakers actually consider utility is irrelevant.
- C. This is out of scope, the argument is not concerned with how much thought cabinetmakers give to the utility of their products.
- D. **Correct**. This option, unlike the other four, provides information that helps fill the gap in the argument.
- E. The issue of monetary value is never raised. This is out of scope.

The correct answer is D.

65.

- A. This would not support Fanto's decision to delay advertising for six months.
- B. This is out of scope but if anything does not support Fanto's decision to delay advertising for six months.
- C. **Correct**. This identifies a reason for Fanto to delay advertising for six months. Its profits might be adversely affected by an early start to advertising.
- D. This would not support Fanto's decision to delay advertising for six months.
- E. This is out of scope, other segments of the industry are not part of the argument. If anything, this would support an argument that Fanto should advertise as soon as possible, to raise awareness for the other segments of the industry.

The correct answer is C.

Printed in Great Britain
by Amazon.co.uk, Ltd.,
Marston Gate.